THE
SUTRA
ON THE
MOUNT

*An Exercise in Nonduality for
Rediscovering the Sermon on the Mount*

TOTO TAY

The Sutra on the Mount

First Edition

ISBN: 979-8-9926459-1- 0

Toto Tay

In *The Sutra on the Mount,* Toto offers a beautiful re-envisioning of the greatest words of Jesus through the lens of dharma traditions. This invigorating interpretation invites those still captivated by the Sermon on the Mount into a new and practical perspective.

- Jory Pryor, author of *Becoming All Light: The Non-Dual Heart of Christianity*

This book, *The Sutra on the Mount,* is for people searching for the joy of the here-and-now Divine presence. Or, maybe they're longing to find the meaning in the religious rituals they practice, but can't find it. It's for people who read the beatitudes of Jesus and can't figure out how being poor, meek, or persecuted can be happy about it. It's for people who try to dig beneath the surface of the Sermon on the Mount (or in the Plain), but they wind up feeling like dogs chasing their tails instead.

Toto Tay has a remarkable way of uncovering healing treasures in Jesus' teachings. Too often Jesus' guide to the Ultimate Reality is interpreted as a cause for blame, shame, and condemnation. But Toto Tay discerns the path that is lit up with unselfish love and sincerity. Walking on this path feels safe, wise, inspiring—and frankly, life-changing.

- Shirley Paulson, author of *Illuminating the Secret Revelation of John: Catching the Light* and primary producer of the blog, podcast, and online courses for Early Christian Texts: The Bible and Beyond

Dedication

To all the ones along the journey
(whether they're aware of it or not)
to a place that's not a place
and where they've always been—
this is for you.

Table of Contents

The Sutra on the Mount

Introduction

I can already hear it in my head: "Whoa, whoa, whoa. What do you mean 'sutra' here, bub?" And honestly, it's a fair question. I chose the term *sutra* deliberately, as a play on words to show how the Sermon on the Mount can be explored from a different point of view. I admit it, as one that might catch people off guard.

Traditionally, the word *sutra* is used in Buddhism and Hinduism to describe a concise precept or teaching. In Sanskrit, it means "thread." I really like the term, as it also suggests that there's an interconnectedness that should be taken into account.

When I look at what Jesus taught–especially his Sermon on the Mount and similar Sermon on the Plain–it seems to me that Jesus practiced a kind of *midrash* just as many teachers of the Tanakh (Hebrew scriptures) would have done. The word comes from Hebrew *miḏrāš*, meaning to make commentary on, and *dāraš*, to investigate and expound. As a method, it allows one to dive deeply into the life and spirit of a text beyond the surface appearance of its words.

In big and small ways, we do this quite naturally with Scripture, which could easily explain the sheer number of tens of thousands of differing denominations today. I recently read the latest count was around 45,000 or so. Whatever the exact number is, it's certainly nothing to shake a stick at. And have you ever noticed how many Biblical commentaries there are out there, investigating and explaining the various texts? It, too, is a staggering stack that suggests several points of view.

No doubt, different writers have different insights and opinions even over the very same few words of a verse. This diversity

1

of interpretations rang true even within the gospels and epistles in the New Testament themselves. Differences can be found within these two sermons as well, from Matthew's and Luke's accounts that we're about to explore.

I should tell you now that I've encountered God in countless places that fall outside the box of traditional Christianity, and I strongly believe what Jesus learned from "his Father" and shared with crowds was not his exclusive. God is self-revealing to any who seek. And what I still long for–and what I deeply need–is a living connection: one that reflects intimacy, transformation, and transcendence. Even beyond the historical Jesus, Christ embodies exactly that.

In my case of practicing *midrash*, I like to approach passages in the Bible from different angles. I have to explore perspectives that go beyond the interpretation merely told to me, beyond the singular one "right" facet I've been presented with much of my life. I have to step back and look from other viewpoints that also sparkle as Christ for me.[1]

One of the lenses I view things through is that of nonduality. The other tools I use to dig, extract, and polish these gems include insights from a variety of religious traditions. Remember? Christ keeps showing up for us everywhere.

So, what's nonduality? It literally means "not two." The understanding here is that reality is not composed of independent and separate entities. Conceptually, it emphasizes oneness, interconnectedness, and unity in all things beyond

---

[1] As I continued to write this book from this point, I had no original intention of making it into an indictment against Christianity, but I also cannot ignore that at times it may lean in that direction. Of course, this stands alongside the good company of many godly writers since orthodoxy's inception. So, I make no apologies for anything that diverges from tradition as long as it aligns with what Jesus taught.

objects and phenomena. It challenges the dualistic perception of the world as good and bad, subject or object, self and other, sacred and secular, inviting us into a deeper awareness, one in which all things are held together in the mystery of wholeness.

That's not to say we're all the same, or that all spiritual paths are equal. I also don't believe this material world is all just an illusion either, or an overly sophisticated computer program (Sorry, Neo). Appearances and beliefs differ vastly, obviously. It's just that instead of there being separate parts and pieces, there is an experienced cohesion of the Divine being expressed and imbuing all of it, in and as all of it.

So, whether we call it Pure Awareness, Consciousness, Ultimate Reality, the True Self, Shiva, YHWH, God, Christ, or any of 99 or a thousand names, still words fall absurdly flat.

Just as Jesus spoke on the mountainside, and again down on the plain, my invitation to you, dear reader, is this: when He said, "You have heard that it was said to those in ancient times... but I say to you," it was a call to release what no longer serves, to let go of assumptions and projections. So that's what we'll do.

I guess I could've just as easily called this the Sermon on the Coast. These teachings carry vibrations, like waves washing up onto the shore, lingering for a moment on the thirsty sand before pulling back in rhythm, and returning with another wash, slowly smoothing our sharp edges over time.

But for now, the *"Sutra" on the Mount* will work just fine.

Chapter One

It feels most fitting that I begin with this prayer: The Gayatri Mantra.[2]

ॐ भूर्भुवः स्वः
तत्सवितुर्वरेण्यं
भर्गो देवस्यं धीमहि।
धियो यो नः प्रचोदयात्॥

om bhūr bhuvaḥ svaḥ
tat savitur vareṇyaṃ
bhargo devasya dhīmahi
dhiyo yo naḥ pracodayāt

Translation

We meditate upon that most adored Om, I AM, our Creator
and the Source of all life,
Whose Radiant Splendor illuminates all realms,
be they physical, mental or spiritual.
May this Divine Light be that by which we perceive,
which inspires our understanding.[3]

---

[2] Ṛgveda 03.062.10. The Gayatri Mantra is a hymn of atonement that dates back to a time before Moses was most likely even born. It's cited throughout many other Hindu scriptures, liturgies, and ceremonies as well.

[3] The translation is my own from Sanskrit and several English translations, but the hymn itself has been translated by a host of translators, in a wide variety of ways. Even "literal" word for word translations vary greatly, just by how nuanced our languages and dialects are. This could even be an example of *midrash*, which can serve us well within the Bible and in prayer/ meditation, too, as long as we're not so rigid that we break.

4

Toto Tay

I'm sorry if it's too much to start off a book about Jesus' teachings with the 3,000 year-old prayer from a non-Christian tradition.

Should it simply be too big a bite right now, you can ease your way into the book with a prayer from Paul. He offers this right at the beginning of his letter to the Ephesians:

> *That the God of our Lord Jesus Christ,*
> *the Father of glory, may give you a spirit of wisdom*
> *and revelation as you come to know him, so that, with*
> *the eyes of your heart enlightened, you may perceive...* [4]

Aren't those great?

Now as we're starting off, I won't spend too much time diving into the historical background and reception of the Sermon on the Mount, setting up its significance at the time and throughout the past two thousand years, or how it compares word-for-word, line-by-line with the Sermon on the Plain and how the two differ, at least, not in some grand info-dump right at the outset.

Honestly, there's no shortage of books that do that quite well enough.

---

[4] The passage shown is from the letter to the Ephesians. The convention of verses was added for our convenience, but the manuscript itself has neither numerations nor punctuation marks. So, it seems to start in verse 17 and stop after barely setting foot in verse 18 in chapter one. Is there something leading up to this? Yup. Does it continue to specify what we will perceive? Also yup. Am I being super selective like those I accuse of cherry-picking? Nah, not really. I don't deny that there's more, and I don't deny that Paul may have had a different intention than me. This is merely how I negotiated the text in order to hold it up to the Light and see what sparkles for me.

The translation I'm using here and anywhere else in the book is from the New Revised Standard Version Updated Edition, unless stated otherwise.

5

The Sutra on the Mount

What interests me here is an introspective question. How can we approach these teachings–arguably the most well-known and quoted of Jesus' words–and read them in ways that uncover fresh, nourishing insights? My encouragement to you is that any time you open the Bible or any other spiritual text, begin with asking yourself: What do 'I' see in the text–not what I was taught or thought it said before–and WHY?

As I explained in the introduction, one method that Jesus himself seemed to exercise this tradition that presented texts and teachings that could hold multiple meanings, a built-in flexibility that allowed YHWH to reveal new truths directly and personally. This would be how the early Church Fathers (and Mothers) would have interpreted their Scriptures as well.

That's why it's vitally important to acknowledge just how much changes, sometimes drastically, from teacher to oral transmission, to written account, to hand copying texts, to reinterpretation, to translations from completely different languages (and this one really cannot be understated), to appropriating (or misappropriating) the texts that made it in the canon, to (finally) the Scripture we're currently reading.

So, how do we handle the Bible in light of all this? What can we trust? Well, there's something to say about going back to the earliest transmission of the text. Nope, keep going... Further... Further... All the way to the earliest copies (of the copies of copies) in Greek, which, I know, is still a few hundred years and several degrees away from the words coming out of Jesus' mouth. But it's the best we've got.

Now you might be thinking, *What?! How on God's plastic-coated, toxically polluted, not-flat, green earth is that close enough?!* [5]

Fair question. And I'll tell ya why: Because it's not a god-level caricature from a dead chunk of papyrus we're trying to conjure up here. This ain't no séance or LARP session.

First, I have to explain the term *theopneustos* (θεόπνευστος), often translated as "God-breathed," including how it has long been misunderstood. The problematic theology[6] of Biblical inerrancy and infallibility grew from this misunderstanding. But a closer look suggests a richer meaning, something more like "lifegiving," similar to how a good pair of boots (or more accurately, well-fitting sandals) gave life and support to a long walk in ancient times.

Scripture, then, isn't a fossil; it's a refreshment! What we draw from it can be like a tall glass of iced tea on a scorching day. *Ahhhhh!*

How is that? It's because the Divine interpenetrates everything. Yet as errant and fallible as humans and our endeavors are, what gets overlooked is this: the Living God–

---

[5] Yup. Copies of copies of copies, et cetera. There's plenty of books and scholarly papers that go into the details of this, too many to cite. But if you'd like something easily accessible and thoroughly cited, Wiki does a pretty good job here.

https://en.wikipedia.org/wiki/Biblical_manuscript

[6] In the book, The Invention of Inspired Text, John Poirier fantastically tracing the use of the word *theopneustos* from 2 Timothy 2:16 (stating how Scripture is "God-inspired") to a host of Pre-Origen, typical uses meaning "life-giving." Poirier does an excellent job countering Benjamin Warfield's argument that the Bible is the very Word of God Himself and holds the ultimate authority, influencing contemporary evangelism. Of course, the "Bible" wasn't even a thing during the writing of the second letter to Timothy—which also wasn't even written by Paul.

So, there's that…

who is beyond all–also self-limits His/Herself, choosing to be revealed not through perfection, but through Presence.

Despite our mistranslations, misinterpretations, and mistakes, God still speaks. It's not that the words on the page are themselves holy or spoken directly by God, but that God speaks deeply to the heart of an earnest seeker, even through the poor limitations of language.

The Creator of all things meets each of us, along with all of creation, right where we are. Let's face it, a God who isn't accessible to everyone–at any stage of life, in any cultural context, and at every level of understanding–isn't a good God. Nor are they worthy of our attention or affection.

But I believe in a good God. An indescribably good God really. So, back to how exactly one approaches the Bible and other sacred writings, and explores what the writers understood about God in them. Maybe you and I could try a modern twist on *midrash*. Something like this:

Step one: Take the brave effort of making ancient language make sense for today. Most of us aren't fishermen, shepherds, or vintners like people in biblical times. We rarely run into lions, and very few of us ride horseback and shoot with a bow. And sure, we may suffer political strain like they did, but now it is quite different than a world where one wrong move could land you in a stadium facing a gladiator or a wild beast.

So, let's take time to unpack the points Jesus may have been trying to make in ways we can better grasp. We'll be choosing related yet relevant terms to switch out where it's needed. (Think of how The Message translation rephrases the New Testament.)

Step two: We really need to unhitch ourselves from the harmonized caricature of Jesus we've carried in our minds. We must face the fact that there truly are differences between the gospels, Paul's letters, and other Christian writings. It's not one congruent point of view.

Each author had their own perspective, intent, audience, and historical/cultural context. All valid, don't worry. They're just not the same with each other, and definitely not the same as us. Still, we can approach these writings without dragging in all the usual assumptions. We really can (and should) take in these teachings and stories as they are, on their own terms.

To help with this, we may occasionally need to swap out some of these religious buzzwords. Those terms often carry modern baggage and have lost rhythm with their original meanings.

Like I said, I'm using the lens of nonduality simply because that's what draws my attention within these stories. I'm hoping as you listen closely, with the ears of your own heart, different things will likely jump out for you, too. That's how it's supposed to work.

So, just to review.

Step one: Think about it relative to how it makes sense for today. That's when it matters to us. Right now.

Step two: Glide forward with the clarity that comes from the right context, from stories standing on their own, and avoid if at all possible the presumptions and projections that we're often unaware that we do.

Chapter Two

Are we liking these two-counts? Another to consider might be this.

- Take the passage and break it down; then
- Spend some time reflecting in order to create your own arrangement of the piece.

To walk through what I'm talking about in doing this midrash-style method ourselves, and what we'll soon be doing with the Sermon on the Mount (and Sermon on the Plain), I'll start with Paul's prayer as the current piece to work with. Sometimes for this kind of deep dive, I find it helpful to enlist a good interlinear Bible to support the process.[7]

> ἵνα ὁ θεὸς τοῦ κυρίου ἡμῶν Ἰησοῦ Χριστοῦ ὁ πατὴρ τῆς δόξης δώῃ ὑμῖν πνεῦμα σοφίας καὶ ἀποκαλύψεως ἐν ἐπιγνώσει αὐτοῦ πεφωτισμένους τοὺς ὀφθαλμοὺς τῆς διανοίας ὑμῶν εἰς τὸ εἰδέναι ὑμᾶς τίς

The English word-for-word transliteration puts it like this:

> That the God of-the of-Lord of-us of-Jesus of-Christ the father of-the of-glory he-may-give to-you spirit of-wisdom and of-discovery into to-recognition of-him having-been- enlightened the eyes of-the of-heart of-you into the to-have-seen you what?

Now let's switch metaphorical seats and channel our inner sound engineer, pulling our chair up to the mixing board. (See what I did there? "Channel?") Let's bring down the dogma, adjust the dial on terminology, and boost the elucidation. Uh

---

[7] I really like the one Abarim Publications offers online. The BibleHub, too, has several interlinears. Shown above is from the Stephanus Textus Receptus 1550. https://biblehub.com/tr/

oh, we might also want to be careful that our tone isn't too sharp or too flat. (All right, I'll put the puns on pause.)

Let's start with breaking it down: "That the God of-the of-Lord of-us of-Jesus of-Christ…"

At the very beginning, the first musical note, so to say, is the term "God." We don't have to be super picky about every word, and I'm not attacking it. But there might be a tad to be gained by its overall cultural context. And what would that be? It's helpful to me to note that the audience was in Ephesus, a port town on the Aegean Sea across from Athens. During the time of Paul, it would have been booming as a very hot spot for commerce and religion for Christian and pagan alike. It was also home to the Temple of Artemis, one of the Seven Wonders of the World. That's context worth noting, don't ya think?

You see, the meaning of God is nuanced and complicated, and it means something slightly (or not so slightly) different to every ear that hears the word. But it would not have been unusual for at least one of the concepts of God for some during antiquity to indicate the Source and Wholeness of the All, something bigger than what we'd expect. That's the orientation I'll be using, too, as I make this prayer my own.

Next we read, "Of our Lord Jesus Christ." I can recognize that Paul and I have differing perspectives on this figure. His view highlights the mediator between God and humankind. Jesus, himself, was the Immortal Son of God and a human being simultaneously, which granted him unique authority in both heaven and earth. Paul's Jesus was a "bridge" allowing the two realms to connect. (This bridge part, I can sort of see; I don't judge that, I just think we all have that capacity.)

If that speaks to you, that's great. But for me, the "lordship" concept doesn't quite land. I don't experience Jesus in a hierarchical or emissarial way. Instead, I feel a deeply intimate, unitive Presence expressed through what I would call his "Christic" nature. So personally, I resonate with that expression more.

I know I'm sounding awfully fussy, but this is all about the example of how I use sacred texts in my practice, and in this case, interpreting the prayer to make it meaningful. I have to either be real or fake it. So here I am, being real… and yes, a little nitpicky.

Just one more thing: I'm not especially fond of how "father of the glory" has been translated. It tends to evoke imagery of grandeur and fame, like an emperor, only immortal. That depiction pulls the Divine too far from the more Hebraic understanding of Shekinah, the radiant Presence that overflowed from the Temple, that is full of wholeness, compassion, and truth. So, I may rework the line into something more in that spirit. The next part, however, is pretty solid:

May God "give to you a spirit of wisdom and of discovery into the recognition of Him."

I don't plan to change much here, maybe just smooth out the phrasing slightly. I'll sit with it in meditation and see what emerges. Silence has such a beautiful voice.

What comes to mind here is echoed by the Hindu concept of *prajñā*, True Awareness that transcends knowledge. It's the deep realization of one's connection to Ultimate Reality. I especially love the choice of the word "discovery." It evokes that *ah-ha!* moment of something fresh and unexpectedly beautiful, a wide-eyed joy. Then we get to the literal:

"…having-been-enlightened the eyes of-the of-heart of-you into the to-have-seen you what." (From "… *so that, with the eyes of your heart enlightened, you may perceive*.")

Toto Tay

The clip ends by showing us that through enlightenment, what we truly perceive is not by sensory organs but through *ophthalmos kardia*, the "eyes of the heart." It immediately reminds me of that line from The Little Prince by Antoine de Saint-Exupéry:

"It is only with the heart that one can see rightly; what is essential is invisible to the eye." (Such a great book, right?)

These biblical texts do contain some truly lovely melodies. Feel its beat inside your heart, and you'll be swaying in no time.

Let's return once again to how the standard translation presents Paul's prayer for the Ephesians:

That the God of our Lord Jesus Christ,
the Father of glory, may give you a spirit of wisdom
and revelation as you come to know him, so that, with
the eyes of your heart enlightened, you may perceive...

Honestly, I really like this prayer as it stands. But just for fun, let's see what it becomes when reframed. Here's how I would express it through a nondual lens:

May Divine Presence,
Who is Light shining so very brightly upon you,
draw you into deep Awareness
and gift you with a fresh discovery.
It is with your Heart,
as it gazes upon Oneness,
that you will also perceive.

We'll likely circle back to this after we put everything together, right at the end. Perhaps as an invocation...

Chapter Three

Now, before we get too many feathers ruffled, let's remember what we're doing here, just as we mentioned at the beginning of the last chapter. We're taking time to study, break down the passages, and reflect to see what fresh insights they might hold for us. Not just regurgitating what we grew up thinking, right? Not even how they seemed to us last winter, if we happened to read them then. The important question is this: What does it say to me (or to you) today?

I do want to be perfectly clear about something before we get too far along. First off, you don't have to agree with my take on anything. The truth is that what I studied and even firmly believed ten or twenty years ago might earn a facepalm from me today, maybe a slap from someone else, to boot. But back then, I was doing the best I could with what I knew. And the honest truth is that I trust that others are, too. Grace flows in many directions.

Secondly, you don't have to understand everything. Simply showing up is already doing something good. Yes, building strength, muscle, endurance, and awareness takes time and discipline. But it's equally true that there is no shame in being where you are, at this time, in this body, with whatever you're carrying. We do what we can, when we can. For now, that's plenty. So, if something I say is confusing or doesn't resonate, let it go. If you need to know it, it will find its way back to you. As a reminder of what was mentioned at the beginning of the intro, God spills over into everything and is rather spectacular when it comes to meeting us wherever, at whatever level we are, with endless patience and mercy.

And now that we've got that out of the way, we can sit down together and enjoy the meal before us. But if the Sermon on the Mount itself is our entree, let's start a few hors d'oeuvres.

An interesting and helpful way to explore it is from the perspective of an outsider looking in. And perhaps no one modeled that more powerfully than Mahatma Gandhi.

As Thomas Merton pointed out in his 1964 Ramparts Magazine article: "Gandhi's whole concept of man's relation to his own inner being and to the world objects around him was informed by the contemplative heritage of Hinduism, together with the principles of Karma Yoga which blended, in his thought with the ethic of the Synoptic Gospels and the Sermon on the Mount... 'JESUS DIED IN VAIN,' said Gandhi, 'if he did not teach us to regulate the whole of life by the eternal law of love.'"

That outsider perspective struck me deeply, especially since I hadn't noticed it at all from my earlier evangelical vantage point.[8] Shamal Bhatt's poetry, a favorite of Gandhi's, featured one particular stanza beautifully stating this:

> *For a bowl of water give a goody meal;*
> *For a kindly greeting bow thou down with zeal;*
> *For a simple penny pay thou back with gold;*
> *If thy life be rescued, life do not withhold.*
> *Thus the words and actions of the wise regard;*
> *Every little service tenfold they reward.*
> *But the truly noble know all men as one,*

---

[8] There's a difference between judging from the outside and exploring from within. I need to make that distinction. Too much of my upbringing left me critical of stuff I only knew from secondhand finger-pointers. That's not helpful. There is also the outside view looking in from those who have been excluded or kicked out. That's a tough view they didn't ask for. The outside perspective here is helpful, like a mirror.

The Sutra on the Mount

And return with gladness good for evil done.[9]

Gandhi saw in this poem that same spirit that inspired him from the Sermon on the Mount. It was precisely complementary to his beloved Bhagavad Gita. In fact, each helped him better understand the others. (Often cross-cultural and inter-religious studies will do that.)

This teaching of Jesus profoundly shaped his philosophy of Satyagraha,[10] which focused on *ahimsa*, non-violence and passive resistance. Gandhi believed that his own interpretation of the Sermon on the Mount was adulterated except when he took it as a whole, and stressed his difference with orthodoxy in that the teaching was less directed to the disciples alone than to each and every one. "Why else would it need telling?" The Sermon on the Mount was the essence of Christianity. It stood apart from the Old Testament and even from Paul's later interpretations, which honestly reflected a slightly different experience than what was offered by authors of the gospels.

And Gandhi will get no argument from me.

---

[9] M. K. Gandhi, *An Autobiography OR The Story of My Experiments with Truth* (Ahmedabad: Navajivan Publishing House, First Edition - 1927, Reprint, 2011)

[10] M.K. Gandhi, *The Message of Jesus Christ* (Mumbai: Bharatiya Vidya Bhavan, 1998)

Chapter Four

The Sermon on the Mount can be found in Matthew's Gospel, chapters 5–7. It begins with the Beatitudes and ends with a teaching on "merely hearing versus actually doing." In total, there are 22 aphorisms, maxims, logia, *vākya*, or "sutras" if that's what we'd like to call them, six of which are shared with the Sermon on the Plain[11] found in Luke 6.

The Beatitudes are considered to be Jesus' core teaching, his *magnum opus*, or in French, his *pièce de résistance*. I threw that last geographic reference in because, on my first attempt at finding fresh and deeper meaning within the Beatitudes, I was inspired by the French-Algerian Israeli scholar André Chouraqui's translation from *La Bible*.[12] He interprets "blessed" as *en marche!* ("March on!")

---

[11] Aside from the number of aphorisms, the Sermon on the Mount (SOTM) and the Sermon on the Plain (SOTP) have differences in their setting (obviously), their audience and general tone.

In general, SOTM seems to be speaking to a crowd even though his disciples also come up to him, too. It also has a more Jewish flavor to it, with more of an emphasis on personal character and purity, perfection, or spiritual integrity. It feels a bit prompted by the Pharisees—and even his own disciples—over how he handles his "ministry."

SOTP, however, has a more concise and tangible, more merciful tone, and kind of seems more directed at his disciples. The focus here leans more towards social justice and caring for the marginalized, even taking some punches at the oppressors (socio-political and religious).

Even though it appears that more of these instructions are given in the SOTM than in SOTP, it should be noted that most are actually still found later on throughout Luke's gospel. So, they're not really "missing" from either gospel, even though their sequence and settings differ.

Last thing. Some will insist that these are two separate occasions to account for their differences. But I honestly believe that we cannot afford to discount how both occur at the mount (one going up, one coming down), both start with the beatitudes, both end on the same story, and both are immediately followed by Jesus healing the centurion's slave/servant. Dude, it's the same.

[12] See Appendix One for André Chouraqui's original translation.

And it is in that spirit that I first considered how it might be reframed. It was years before coming across *midrash*, and when I started using this method along with my meditation and with *lectio divina*, it felt familiar. So I went back and found it in order to share it here.

(From Matthew 5:3-12)

(Blessed are the poor in spirit, for theirs is the kingdom of heaven.)

> *When you find yourself humbled by the Light of Consciousness, hold steady. You are in the very place where the Divine lives and moves.*

(Blessed are those who mourn, for they will be comforted.)

> *To those who ache with the sorrow felt by others, stay with it. You, too, will be comforted and healed.*

(Blessed are the meek, for they will inherit the earth.)

> *When your heartmind[13] leads you into being more selfless, gentle and kind, keep it up. You'll find balance and harmony within yourself in this world.*

(Blessed are those who hunger and thirst for righteousness, for they will be filled.)

---

[13] As I explained in *The Teacher, The Twin, & The Tower*, "in Chinese philosophy, the concept of *xin* (心) combines both the heart and mind, literally "heartmind." It's the idea that understanding, intention, and one's feeling about something are all from one space. Emotions without intellect or using reason without reading the mood is a sign of an undeveloped or fragmented cognition.

Toto Tay

To those roused by a deep longing for virtue and decency, march on! Justice and integrity walk beside you.

(Blessed are the merciful, for they will receive mercy.)

When you tend to those in need of mercy, trust that it flows directly from the Source, who is stirred with deep compassion for you and through you.

(Blessed are the pure in heart, for they will see God.)

Hold fast, you who know what wholeness means. Consciousness has been revealed to you and will continue to guide your way.

(Blessed are the peacemakers, for they will be called children of God.)

To you who stand in solidarity with peace itself, connected to all things and all people, feel the full strength in your legs and the steadiness in your steps. You are the Manifestation of True Reality.

(Blessed are those who are persecuted for the sake of righteousness, for theirs is the kingdom of heaven.)

If you find yourself mistreated or targeted for your commitment to integrity and ethical living, keep moving forward. The Divine is wholly committed to you and walks with you.

(Blessed are you when people revile you and persecute you and utter all kinds of evil against you falsely on my account. Rejoice and be glad, for your reward is great in heaven, for in the same way they persecuted the prophets who were before you.)

The Sutra on the Mount

So, when this happens, march on. You are standing, even now, in your True Self. You will find bliss in Consciousness, just as the enlightened ones have throughout time.

Chapter Five

Like I said, I carried this rendering with me into meditation and reflection, and it's something I still return to, again and again, in my practice. But part of *midrash*, in my understanding, is to take up the gem and gaze a little deeper to see how it sparkles now, in the light of a new day and from a fresh angle.

Each of the eight Beatitudes in Matthew (only half of which appear in Luke) begins with the word *makarios*. It's a word that's quite elusive in meaning. The closest we find in English is the word "untouchable." Not, however, in the usual "ew yuck" kind of way. Nope. *Makarios* is meant to describe the "far beyond" kind of way, exceeding the height one could possibly reach. Imagine the feeling you might have after being served a delicacy, prepared just for you, plated exquisitely on its dazzling dish. It's so scrumptious! It's like nothing even remotely close to what you ever dreamed of.

That's the kind of "untouchable" we're talking about. But somewhere along the way, it got translated as (insert yawn) *"blessed."*

The first exhortation is directed to the "poor in spirit." Who exactly is Jesus talking about here?

Cynthia Bourgeault frames spiritual poverty as the absence of any claim to possess all the right answers. There's nothing you're clinging to; your hands are empty and open to receive.[14] I have always liked this, and that was the understanding I had when I approached the Beatitudes in Chapter Four.

---

[14] Cynthia Bourgeault has a whole section covering the Beatitudes in her book, *The Wisdom Jesus.*

We also find in Luke's version, from the Sermon on the Plain, that it's just "blessed are the poor." (Sometimes, but not always, this shows an earlier version before scribes or other authors elaborate.) If we want to, we can at least start with this smaller chunk.

Most likely, when you or I hear the word "poor," we think about the other side of wealthy and comfortable. The picture in our heads is of somebody who may be struggling to pay rent or mortgage, perhaps unable to get three healthy meals every day, or buy new clothes with any regularity.

But the Greek adjective *ptochos* (πτωχος) means something even more destitute. It's closer to the concept of shrinking away from something or cowering in desperation, as a mouse might do when a hawk swoops down. In the context here, it's used to describe how there are those people whom everyone cringes away from. It refers to their deep shame and a social scorn so thorough, they are considered not just worthless, but something far less. They are needy on a whole other level, completely debilitated, forsaken and scarred. Society has assigned them a somehow negative value.

In his book, *Jesus and the Disinherited*, Howard Thurman describes perfectly what this looks like today, and how Jesus thought and taught from a different attitude than most, even religious folks.[15]

> "I can count on the fingers of one hand the number of times that I have heard a sermon on the meaning of religion, of Christianity, to the man who stands with his back against the wall. It is urgent that my meaning be

---

[15] *Jesus and the Disinherited* is jam packed full of goodness! I would be remiss if I didn't also include a dog-eared page or two I had from it about how divergent the church has become from this, Jesus' most popular sermon. See Appendix Two.

crystal clear. The masses of men live with their backs constantly against the wall. They are the poor, the disinherited, the dispossessed. What does our religion say to them?"

"Living in a climate of deep insecurity, Jesus, faced with so narrow a margin of civil guarantees, had to find some other basis upon which to establish a sense of well-being. He knew that the goals of religion as he understood them could never be worked out within the then-established order. Deep from within that order, he projected a dream, the logic of which would give to all the needful security. There would be room for all, and no man would be a threat to his brother. 'The kingdom of God is within.' 'The Spirit of the Lord is upon me, because he hath anointed me to preach the gospel to the poor.'"

"Blessed are the poor **in spirit**, for theirs is the kingdom of heaven."

Starting from that rock bottom level, let's add *"in spirit"* back in and see if it makes a difference, or if it doesn't really matter.

The word *pneuma* (πνεῦμα) is often associated with "breath," and as such, tends to be slightly over-indexed as "spirit." But a deeper understanding of *pneuma* takes us down to the smallest parts of the body. In today's terms, it could be understood as *atomically*, and not just the particles themselves, but their bonds. Their very connection and relationship are the point. It's what is shared at the molecular level, and it's what sustains life.

Okay. Somehow, we've just gone from a negative value to something even worse. That seems pertinent, so we're definitely holding on to *"in spirit."*

"Blessed are the poor in spirit, **for theirs is the kingdom of heaven.**"

And let's not forget what Jesus meant by *"kingdom of heaven."* For him, it wasn't a location but a space, a state of presence, consciousness, or unified field. It's a realm of shared responsibility and care, grounded in awe and wonder for all that is, for Ultimate Reality itself. It's an eternal moment that includes all invisible and visible existence. And it literally turns the worst destitution upside down and inside out, to the highest and widest and deepest connection and value imaginable. Wow!

Now, let's put it all together and see what we can draw from it:

Sutra 1.1

You, who are so downcast and mistreated that even money can't help you, be exalted! For you share in the Divine and have belonged since before the Beginning of Time.

Chapter Six

I know, I know, five chapters in, and I've barely stepped outside the Christian tradition. *Where's the dharma, bro? You tossed the opening mantra for a blurb from Paul, and even have Gandhi focused on Bible passages!* I'm getting there. No worries.

"Blessed are those who mourn, for they will be comforted."

This kind of mourning in the Beatitudes isn't ordinary grief. It's the powerless, hopeless despair that comes from something being taken away, or never given at all. It hits on a whole different level. It's the thief that steals one's very sense of worth, that makes a person question their existence, that leads them to believe they somehow deserve their pain. Everything hurts, and the ache reaches the deepest part of us, in complete darkness.

These are the ones Jesus is speaking to: *"Behold the Light, and feel its warmth!"*

The other side of this teaching appears in the Sermon on the Plain, paired with a scary "woe":

"Woe to you who are laughing now, for you will mourn and weep.[16]"

There's a verse in the *Isha Upanishad* that speaks to overcoming this kind of sadness or loneliness. It's verse 7, and goes something like this:

यस्मिन् सर्वाणि भूतान्य् आत्मैवाभूद् विजानतः ।
तत्र को मोहः कः शोक एकत्वम् अनुपश्यतः ॥

---

[16] Luke 6:25b

The Sutra on the Mount

yasmin sarvāṇi bhūtāny ātmaivābhūd vijānataḥ |
tatra ko mohaḥ kaḥ śoka ekatvam anupaśyataḥ ||

Translation

*When a knower discovers Oneness, that all beings become
the knower's very self, what delusion of being alone,
what grief, is there left to be sad about?*

One of the reasons that I find Hindu and Buddhist concepts so
resonant is that so much of their focus revolves around the
elimination of suffering. It's always met with grace and
compassion.

When I read Jesus' sermons, Jesus is not like the preachy types,
and his healings are not like the pious types. It's sometimes
hard to imagine what Jesus was actually like, because of how
he's been presented (or misrepresented).

Too often, we're handed the image of the "no crying he makes"
miracle baby Jesus. It follows up with a teenager who one-ups
his biological parents and shows-up the nearly speechless
priests. He's they guy who then grows up into this perfect god-
man who commands with authority, virtually emasculating his
opponents and flipping heavy tables. From a thousand pulpits
is painted the picture of a shoulders-back, chin-up, wise-as-
Solomon, ripped, chiselled–and dare I say, "sexy"–superstar
slash superhero that's saving the day and then some (like all
eternity).

Yet arguably what we read and reflect on seems far more
human, someone who speaks to the broken from the place of
his own brokenness. He comes to those who can't stop crying,
because his own clothes are tear-stained, too. And all of this
tenderness, this overflowing love, comes from his Union with
the Divine, from being one with the Father (or, in Aramaic,

Abwoon, a fusion of *Abba* and *womb*, cosmic birther, beyond masculinity or femininity). The same Divine Oneness that is yours, too.

Sutra 1.2

You, who are hopelessly sad, feeling abandoned and utterly alone, the Divine sees you. Open your eyes and witness how Consciousness is drawing you into the loving embrace of Oneness.

***

The next line can be tricky:

"Blessed are the meek, for they will inherit the earth."

We rarely use the word "*meek*" much, unless it comes up in reference to the Sermon on the Mount.

I remember growing up and hearing pastors say things like, *"People think meekness is weakness, but I'm tellin' ya, it's strength!"* And I remember thinking, *"Seriously? I've never heard anyone say anything with the word 'meek' in it."* I was probably so distracted by that thought that I never even caught how they explained it. (Or if they ever really explained it at all.)

So, what is "meek," really? Let's look at the Greek.

The word *praeis* (πραεῖς), from *praus* (πραΰς), is usually translated as "gentle," "humble," or sometimes "submissive," but it has nothing specifically related to being tamed by another. Rather, meekness is having complete control over yourself and your situation, with calmness and kindness at that.

And what's the result? *"They will inherit the earth."*

Meaning this: these are the ones who will reap the true reward of their investment in others. Harmony is the reward for their sacrifices, and it works on the level of interiorness, too, in one's own struggles. A good heart is healthy for the body. No doubt, generosity and gentleness have physical benefits as well as what they provide for others.

The *Tao Te Ching*, a 4th-century BCE Chinese manuscript on "The Way and Its Power," speaks deeply to this.

In Chapter 67, we read:

> *Everywhere I go, people tell me, "Tao is so powerful, so immense, it's inconceivable!" But it's only powerful because it's inconceivable.*
>
> *If we could wrap our minds around it, Tao would be just another thing.*
>
> *The three most important qualities in life are compassion, or showing kindness and mercy to others; moderation, or knowing what a thing is worth; and modesty, or knowing your place in the world.*
>
> *Courage stems from showing kindness and mercy to others. Generosity starts with knowing what a thing is worth.*
>
> *True leadership begins with knowing your place in the world. But these days, I see everyone trying to act courageous without any trace of compassion.*

They try to be generous, but they don't practice moderation in their own lives. They act like leaders, but they have no sense of modesty.

No good can come of this. If you want to get ahead, show people compassion. When other people attack you, defend yourself with compassion.

It's the most powerful force in the universe.[17]

The Tao Te Ching finishes on the same note with Chapter 81:

The truth isn't flashy. Flashy words aren't true. Educated people aren't always smart. Smart people don't always have an education.

Good people don't argue. People who argue aren't good.

The Masters don't hang on to things. They're always doing something for other people, so they always have more to give.

They give away whatever they have, so what they have is worth more.

If you want to get right with Tao, help other people, don't hurt them.

The Masters always work with people, never against them.

---

[17] This is Ron Hogan's translation. It's a completely modern translation that I find quite fantastic. The *Tao Te Ching* is so subtle. It's beyond poetic or precise language, Chinese, English or otherwise, so why not take this 4th century piece, spend a decade living it like Ron did, and then do your best to let it speak from the heartmind. Like Ron did. I've got over a dozen translations, but I keep coming back to this one.

These principles, written hundreds of years before the Sermon on the Mount, offer a beautiful and resonant understanding of *meekness*.

I also love that Jesus seems to cast a wider net here. The blessings aren't confined to the deeply destitute, but extended to other rungs on the ladder one might find themselves, perhaps Roman citizens or soldiers in the crowd. And we know Pharisees and religious leaders certainly were. There's something here for them, too.

I'm also going to stick (mostly) with my earlier translation of this verse from Chapter Four. Even after digging deeper into the Greek and comparing it with the *Tao*, I just like how it fits with what we're doing.

And as I sit with it, the form may change shape with time, growing alongside my meditation practice. Either way, it still speaks.

Sutra 1.3

When your "heartmind" leads you to be selfless, gentle, and kind, keep going. You'll discover balance and harmony within yourself in this life.

Chapter Seven

What's next? "Blessed are those who hunger and thirst for righteousness, for they will be filled.[18]"

What do we make of this? No doubt, the crowd listening would be all too familiar with physical hunger and thirst. A line like this would surely grab their attention. But then Jesus throws in "for righteousness!", which feels like a bait and switch at first. I mean, here I'm thinking about a bacon cheeseburger and a Dr Pepper, and suddenly the combo meal I was drooling for gets swapped out for–what's that again? Righteousness?

On top of that, the way I was raised to think about righteousness left me with a bad taste in my mouth. The image shoved into our heads was of how pure and holy we had to act. Perhaps in that crowd listening to Jesus, there were a few Goody Two-Shoes like that, but are we really saying Jesus is encouraging his mostly outcast audience with some "chin up, ol' boy, you'll soon be mingling in high society?" It's rather dubious, isn't it?

What's helpful here is understanding that during antiquity, the term "righteous" was typically used in the context of being civilized and socially appropriate, not necessarily pious.

I honestly believe this verse ties back to the previous one– about meekness and being humble, self-controlled, which would be setting the stage for what's coming next.[19] We just saw how even the privileged were urged to be meek, to try leading from below, as they say, through service and mercy.

---

[18] Matthew 5:6

[19] Spoiler alert! Stop here if you wanna be surprised… But I'm talking about the kind of justice that fulfills *all* of the laws: The Law of Love! (Matthew 5:17) *Crack!* And it's outta the park!

Again: "Blessed are those who hunger and thirst for righteousness, for they will be filled."

Maybe now's a good time to explain the concept of *dharma* and why it plays such a big role in Hindu epics like the Mahabharata, from which the Bhagavad Gita comes. It's a fascinating and complex idea. I even considered using *dharma* as the book's title for that very reason.

But for our purposes, the Sermon on the Mount, like *dharma*, encompasses various aspects of social, natural, and internal order, that is, what's meant by "righteousness." These are seen in practices and behaviors that bring liberation from suffering, and like here, how one balances justice with mercy. The term *dharma* comes from the root meaning "to sustain or uphold," which is exactly where the Beatitudes shine.

Teachings from both the Sermon on the Mount and the Bhagavad Gita keep circling back to selfless action, how even the most spiritually gifted aspirant's ascension often begins with physical steps. We're encouraged to consider the balance between individual duties and collective responsibilities, and then to balance our purpose with grace, both for others and ourselves.

Sutra 1.4

You are like no other, guided by integrity, modesty and moderation, courtesy and kindness. Freedom is sure to be your close friend.

***

"Blessed are **the merciful**, for they will receive mercy."

Like righteousness, "mercy" was another term loaded with assumptions. Other than the cry of kids yelling "UNCLE!" or "I GIVE!", it was frequently paired with the attribute of "grace" in clever quips about how mercy was *not* getting what you *deserve*, and grace was getting *something good* you don't *deserve*. The purpose was less about understanding grace or mercy than it was to reinforce the idea that God is "gooder" than good while people are worthless and wicked.

But the ancient meaning of mercy went much deeper. Those who showed mercy, in Greek *eleēmones* (ελεημονες), acted to fill in the gaps for others who struggled to meet such a will but fell short, so they could be on equal ground. In other words, the receiver of mercy had the same heart and longing, and the provider shared from their strength, willing to pull the extra weight.

Jesus was assuring his listeners that those who show mercy will themselves be covered. They, too, will be provided for since they showed a willingness to follow the way themselves, but also helped others to do the same.

I'm holding to the earlier translation I made (from Chapter Four) for this one, too. Sometimes we go unrecognized when we keep pouring from our own cup into the empty cups around us, or it goes unseen. It's not that we make sacrifices just to be noticed (hopefully), but we feel drained and wonder how much longer we can keep it up.

I firmly believe it must be emphasized that God notices when we see one another.

If we're overflowing with God's mercy, it's enough. But if we're just burning our own energy, from our own intentions and agendas, it can run out. And then we burn out.

Sutra 1.5

When you care for those in need of mercy, know with confidence that it flows directly from Source, who is moved by deep, visceral love for you, and through you.

Chapter Eight

"Blessed are **the pure in heart**, for they will see God."

The phrase "pure in heart" has often been overshadowed by the Evangelical push of "purity culture." In an earlier form, there was the Puritan movement led by John Calvin and later Jonathan Edwards. Their Protestant vision leaned heavily on moralism and hard work, shaping much of what today is known as "American Christianity."

But the purity Jesus spoke of wasn't about being flawless or maintaining appearances. Yes, it required some effort, a good internal cleaning, but only in the sense of becoming a finely tuned, fully functioning being as we were designed to be. It's remarkably similar in meaning to how our cells dynamically work together in health and healing, supporting our capacity to thrive.

The "pure in heart" reflects the same idea as when Jesus rebuked some of the religious folks who confronted him, time after time:

> "Woe to you, scribes and Pharisees, hypocrites! For you clean the outside of the cup and of the plate, but inside they are full of greed and self-indulgence. You blind Pharisee! First clean the inside of the cup and of the plate, so that the outside also may become clean.[20]"

A paraphrase from the Gospel of Thomas shares the same story in this way:

> "Consciousness is sending you a message. It's a free offer that can be redeemed for your True Self. Now, it's

---

[20] Matthew 23:25-26

up to you to release the false *sense* of Self, asking, 'When would you like to come get this imposter? It's all yours.'"

"Do you only wash the outside of your cup? Why is its appearance so important? Who you are matters so much more than just how you seem."

Speaking as the One, the Teacher said, "Come over here. I can help with your heavy load. I can help make your journey a lot easier, and you can finally settle into your rhythm.[21]"

Are you seeing how each of these Beatitudes ties together and intertwines?

It's so beautiful!

Sutra 1.6

To you, who have done the hard work of recognizing Oneness and healing your heart, you will be sustained by the full spectrum of Light.

***

"Blessed are **the peacemakers**," the next part says, "for they will be called children of God.[22]"

---

[21] From *Thom's Gospel* and *The Teacher, The Twin, & The Tower*, by yours truly. Sayings 88 - 90 reframes Christian terms to reflect the contextual, revolutionary way that Jesus taught, with a modern spin of course. (*wink!*)

[22] Matthew 5:9

This part is really interesting to me. I'll tell ya why. Jesus lived smack dab during the middle of the *Pax Romana* ("Roman Peace") era, which was ironically anything but peaceful for most non-Romans. For many, it was a time marked by violence and oppression amid Rome's vast conquests. So, this Beatitude stands in stark contrast to the Roman emperors, often referred to as "sons of God." Yet here's Jesus blessing the crowd of people and disciples with the same title. Now that's really subversive!

We know Jesus wasn't just campaigning for political peace. Nope. Inner peace is the truly transforming kind that we all want and need.

What also fascinates me is that despite Western views of the East as often warring and wartorn, many culturally and traditionally emphasize peace, albeit somewhat subconsciously. Just look at the greetings across the Eastern world. Jews say "shalom," Muslims greet with "salam alaykum," and in India, one is likely to hear an "Om Shanti" here and there that's echoed in Hinduism, Buddhism, and yoga.

Harder in practice than it is an overarching principle, but leading with these salutations isn't such a bad way to start, don't ya think?

The Hindu Upanishads are steeped in peace, both as an inner state and universal ideal, offering meditation, detachment, and self-inquiry as tools. They often direct our attention inward, helping us see the impermanence of external circumstances, which can also bring equanimity and freedom from suffering.

"For they will be called children of God."

This Beatitude also highlights our interconnectedness with all beings and with God, and the unity between the individual self (Atman) and the universal Self (Brahman). When we realize this, we are moved (or God moves through us) in empathy and compassion towards balance, as it should be.

One way this manifests is through numerous peace mantras. Among my favorites is this one:[23]

ॐ असतो मा सद्गमय ।
तमसो मा ज्योतिर्गमय ।
मृत्योर् मामृतं गमय ।
ॐ शान्तिः शान्तिः शान्तिः ॥

om asato mā sadgamaya
tamaso mā jyotirgamaya
mṛtyor mā'mṛtaṃ gamaya
om śāntiḥ śāntiḥ śāntiḥ

Translation[24]

Om! From the unreal, lead me to the real! From the darkness, lead me to the light! From death, lead me to immortality! Om, Peace! Peace! Peace!

It's with mantras like these, chanted for thousands of years by millions of souls, that I find help in my meditation practice to recognize and deeply feel my sense of Oneness. Now, it's simply something I cannot unsee or unfeel.

---

[23] This is also known as the *Pavamana Mantra* (or *pavamāna abhyāroha*). The translation I use the most is from Patrick Olivelle. It's the one I use here, from the *Bṛhadāraṇyaka Upaniṣad* (1.3.28)

[24] There are a bunch of translations of this, and of many ancient texts. A popular one also has the first line as "From falsehood, lead me to Truth." I like this one, too. It's a good habit to explore various translations and meanings to passages to see what jumps out at you, whether they are Biblical or Vedic or whatnot.

Sutra 1.7

To you who stand in solidarity with peace itself, connected with all people and all things, feel the full strength of your legs and steadiness of your feet! You are the Manifestation of True Reality.

Chapter Nine

The section of the Beatitudes ends on this note:

> Blessed are those who are persecuted for the sake of righteousness, for theirs is the kingdom of heaven.[25]

Often, people read this and think of martyrs throughout history (fewer in number than we'd assume, but still seen as heroic role models), or they misappropriate a modern "suffering for Jesus". Often, however, many just play the victim as they're being called out for hypocrisy and privilege. We can't just cry "I'm persecuted for my faith" for being aggressive, oppressive, annoying, or upset that someone disagrees with us.

So, we might ask: is there a group today this Beatitude actually speaks to? Definitely, and ironically, it's often the last group we were talking about that's doing the persecuting. Sadly, this has been the case for the past 1,700 years.

"Blessed are those who are persecuted for the sake of righteousness..."

There it is again, "righteousness." Remember how it was more to do with being ethical and socially appropriate? And what would righteousness look like today, in the 21st century? Let's break it down:

Respect and Empathy.

Showing respect for others' opinions, beliefs, and identities is a must. And yes, especially when they differ from your own. The ability to understand and

---

[25] Matthew 5:10

share others' feelings (that's what we mean by "empathy"), is also key.

Inclusivity and Diversity.

Recognizing and valuing diversity in all its forms (this includes race, ethnicity, gender, sexual orientation, and ability). It's increasingly important for communities to thrive.

Critical Thinking and Digital Literacy.

Seriously, being able to critically and accurately evaluate information, especially in this digital age, is crucial. This includes spotting misinformation and biases, and calling out disinformation (respectfully, like the first thing here).

Effective Communication.

It's basic, I know, but vital. We have to foster clear, respectful, and constructive communication, in person and online. Active listening, constructive feedback, and avoiding generalizations or stereotypes are absolutely essential.

Civic Engagement.

Participating in your community and society is socially appropriate. A healthy community includes volunteering, activism, and engaging one another in informed discussions. It's a kind of practice what you preach opportunity.

Environmental Awareness.

A well-adjusted society recognizes the importance of environmental issues and takes steps to reduce negative impacts. After all, we all live here. This should be a given.

Adaptability and Lifelong Learning.

Education and a love for learning are vital. The world constantly changes (yes, change is hard, so getting used to it helps). Being adaptable and open to new things is essential.

Professionalism.

In the workplace, being punctual, reliable, and respectful matters, both towards our colleagues and clients. This message is brought to you by HR. And your mom.

Personal Responsibility.

This should be obvious since it appears in nearly every example here. But it really is the only way for a family, a business, a neighborhood, a country, or anything to function effectively. Taking responsibility for our decisions as well as our actions is how we stand, or else we fall. "It starts with me," right?

Nine wonderful tasks to help turn things around. (Sorry, not sorry for getting on a soapbox there.)

Some might be thinking, or perhaps even loudly screaming, "Whoa, what's with these nine points of *wokeness*?"

And we'd reply, "What if we make it ten then. Kind of like the Ten Commandments?" (*wink!*)

Avoid Dissension and Conspiracies.

Throughout history, these never end well. Besides, they fly in the face of everything Jesus taught. Just look at what we've been reading, and stay tuned for much more!

I grew up in an Evangelical home, church at least three times a week, Christian school, and volunteering whenever possible. We read Christian books and listened to Christian music. All our friends and acquaintances were Christian. And everyone else was "in the world."

While we were taught the world doesn't understand or value our spiritual commitment, even though some may have mocked or avoided us, I hesitate to call it "persecution." More often, those outside our fellowship (tribe, cult, or whatever you want to call it) were probably uncomfortable with our corporately holier-than-thou attitude. They were understandably resistant (though I didn't get it then) to our proselytizing and indignation.

I had no clue how seemingly oblivious I was to Jesus' attitude toward those different from him. We put him on a pedestal and thought we could claim "his sacrifice on our behalf" to join the "chosen" club. In this subtle way (sometimes less than subtle), we looked down on others and thought in our minds that it was justifiably so.

But time and again, Jesus healed those who felt abandoned and looked down upon. He taught about serving "the least of these." And he went to his death without resistance, showing us how to let it all go.

It wasn't meant for us to cash in on treasures in heaven, using his credit card through substitutionary atonement.[26] Nope. It

---

[26] Swami Sarvapriyananda used this line, quoting a friend of his. I love it, and I'm rewarded by its cleverness. It's something that really sticks.

was to show us that whatever we think we gain by "belonging to the Kingdom" is something all humans already have.

He, and we, are here to lift others up and remind them.

Sutra 1.8

If you find yourself being targeted or mistreated because of your commitment to integrity and virtue, keep on going. The Divine walks with you is fully committed to your path.

Because you stand as your True Self, you will find bliss in Consciousness, just as all of the enlightened ones have throughout all time.

Chapter Ten

This is where what we call the Beatitudes end. But in the manuscript, his sermon continues within the same event.

Next, Jesus uses the analogy of salt.[27]

> "You are the salt of the earth, but if salt has lost its taste, how can its saltiness be restored? It is no longer good for anything but is thrown out and trampled underfoot."

However, the Gospel of Mark, considered the earliest of the synoptic gospels, adds this after a "fiery" diatribe:

> "If any of you cause one of these little ones who believe in me to sin, it would be better for you if a great millstone were hung around your neck and you were thrown into the sea. If your hand causes you to sin, cut it off; it is better for you to enter life maimed than to have two hands and be thrown into hell, to the unquenchable fire. And if your foot causes you to sin, cut it off; it is better for you to enter life lame than to have two feet and be thrown into hell. And if your eye causes you to sin, tear it out; it is better to enter the kingdom of God with one eye than to have two eyes and be thrown into hell, where their worm never dies and the fire is never quenched.

---

[27] Matthew 5:13 Also in Luke's account, although not where we'd expect in his Sermon on the Plain, but later and at the end of chapter 14. Like we've said before, some of the teachings in the Sermon on the Mount from Matthew are duplicated in the Sermon on the Plain from Luke, and other similar teachings are in scenes later in Luke's account.

"For everyone will be salted with fire. Salt is good, but if salt has lost its saltiness, how can you season it? Have salt in yourselves and be at peace with one another.[28]"

What the literal hell/Gehenna, man! We all know (or just learned right here) that Mark's account likely informed Matthew and Luke. Why does Mark have this extra context to the salt metaphor? Was it added later, like the controversial ending of Mark?[29] Perhaps.

But we can still work with it.

Let's set this up. The phrase translated as "causes you to sin" (some versions say causes you to stumble, offends you, is a snare, or irritation) is Greek word *skandalizo* (σκανδαλίζω). Like "scandalize?" Yup. But what this meant precisely, however, related to night fishing. You read that right. I said "night fishing." Remember now, most of Jesus' disciples were career fishermen, and others would have been familiar with what he implied here. Of course, we need it explained.

The real instruction is this: don't use a false light to deceive others, especially those just starting out. Apparently, it's better to jump overboard, at night no doubt, plunging into darkness and drowning there than to lead others astray with a fake divine insight.

If you try to trick people into following the path with an artificial light, that is, by manipulation or faking your own

---

[28] Mark 9:42-50

[29] It is interesting, huh. This actually sounds closer to what the author of Matthew would've said, but it's not recorded there. The better speculation is that this is one of those parts that was added later than the copies the authors of Matthew and Luke had, similar to what we see in Mark 16:9-20, added in the late 2nd century. (In itself, a bit of a scandal, huh.) But like I said, it doesn't mean we can't work with it. In fact, we might even learn a thing or two.

journey, that's really bad. Instead, you just need to slow down, face your own struggles, and get on the right path.

And if something distracts you? Get rid of it! Toss it into the stinky, burning trash heap. That's what our reference to Gehenna means, not Dante's Inferno. There's no underworld where the wicked live forever with tormenting demons. Gehenna was a real place outside the city, like a primitive dump.

Although Gehenna did have historical significance before Jesus as the Valley of Hinnom, a place Jews saw as desecrated by child sacrifice rituals. And when Jesus said whatever part of you that wants to take the easy, misleading, hypocritical way, that's the part that will end up defiling you if not discarded. So chunk that thing! Throw it far away, where it belongs, in the nastiest place you can imagine.

So, that's the context Mark sets for the salt analogy and where Jesus takes it. (Aren't we glad we decided to work with it?)

Yet here with salt itself is another misunderstanding, thanks to some sloppy glossing. Jesus wouldn't lead with all this scandalous stuff, only to twist the salt metaphor as something like, "Be bold with your seasoning, make your chips and salsa tasty! Nobody likes it bland.[30]"

You see, the point about salt was never about flavor, but about purification and preservation. Jesus' teaching doesn't suddenly turn spicy. That's nonsense. What does align with both Mark and the Beatitudes is this: I will salt you, as in decontaminate you, and heal you by extracting moisture (another function of

---

[30] Quick note about salt in antiquity: It was a commodity. So, if it was good in quality, it held a high value. If it had "lost its saltiness," it was literally both useless and worthless, in functionality and value; in context, it was *fiat money*, backed by nothing... kind of like the American dollar now.

salt; but what moisture? Maybe our birth water, or even baptism) with my Fire.[31]

Marguerite Porete, a 13th-century Beguine and Christian mystic, writes:[32]

> "Now this Soul, says Love, is so burned in Love's fiery furnace that she has become very fire, so that she feels no fire, for in herself she is fire, through the power of Love which has changed her into the fire of Love. This fire burns of and through itself, everywhere, incessantly, without consuming any matter or being able to wish to consume it, except only from itself..."

Now that's being salted by Fire.

Sutra 2.1

Through you, the Divine cleanses the wounds of the world. As Consciousness is recognized, it is set ablaze. The purification and preservation you receive extend to all you touch.

---

[31] I find fire to be an interesting metaphor. It gets me thinking about John the Baptist's "I baptize you with water for repentance (*metanoia*, think from the bigger viewpoint) He will baptize you with the Holy Spirit and fire." (Matthew 3:11)

In Thomas 82 (that is, the Gospel of Thomas Saying 82), Jesus is saying, "Whoever is near me is near the fire, and whoever is far from me is far from the kingdom." (translation by Mark Mattison)

It tracks. Doesn't it?

[32] From *The Mirror of Simple Souls*

Chapter Eleven

And where there's Fire, there's Light. Amirite?

The Sermon on the Mount continues with this:[33]

> "You are the light of the world. A city built on a hill cannot be hid. People do not light a lamp and put it under the bushel basket; rather, they put it on the lampstand, and it gives light to all in the house. In the same way, let your light shine before others, so that they may see your good works and give glory to your Father in heaven."

The same passage found in the Gospel of Thomas puts it this way:[34]

> Jesus said, "A city built and fortified on a high mountain can't fall, nor can it be hidden."

> Jesus said, "What you hear with one ear, listen to with both, then proclaim from your rooftops. No one lights a lamp and puts it under a basket or in a hidden place. Rather, they put it on the stand so that everyone who comes and goes can see its light."

And it continues with this:[35]

> Jesus said, "If someone who's blind leads someone else who's blind, both of them fall into a pit."

Before we put all this together, let's break down the parts.

---

[33] Matthew 5:14-16

[34] Thomas 32 & 33 (Mattison)

[35] Thomas 34 (Mattison)

"You are the light of the world," or *kosmos* (κοσμος), not in the outer space sense of cosmos we usually think of, but meaning the "order" or civilized, cultural setting you live in.

That is to say, it's on you to reflect the Light for those around you. And there's no hiding it. (All the more reason to be decontaminated, shiny, and clean, eh?)

As the rendering of the Gospel of Thomas put it,[36]

> "You shouldn't feel like you have to hide it, but show how you know it, as well! It would be useless to hook up a porch light only to cover it and never turn it on. No! You put it right on the Path, so others can see it clearly and move along safely."

The Gospel of Thomas has a lot to say about Light. Saying 50 is one of my favorites! The first part goes like this:

> Jesus said, "If they ask you, 'Where do you come from?' tell them, 'We've come from the light, the place where light came into being by itself, established itself, and appeared in their image.'"

I also love what Abbot George Burke (Swami Nirmalananda Giri) had to say about this:[37]

> "We enter this relative field of evolution from 'the place where the light came into being on its own accord and established itself and became manifest through their image.' That is the point at which the Invisible

---

[36] In both *Thom's Gospel* and *The Teacher, The Twin, & The Tower*, I use a translation technique that is called "transpositioning" to come up with a modern rendering of the Gospel of Thomas. It more or less focuses on the original cultural context and meaning rather than literally swapping terms word-for-word. This is from Saying 33.

[37] From *The Gospel of Thomas for Awakening,*

Light became Visible Light so creation could be projected for our habitation and evolution. That Light manifested as the creation in which we too became manifest. Being images of God, we became revelations of God just as the sun is reflected in many vessels of water."

"The reflections are many, but the Reflected is One."

And if we consider the end of this passage from Thomas along with this part in the Sermon on the Mount, it makes sense. It also connects with the warning from Mark just before about using artificial light. If we can't see by the Light ourselves, we will only lead others astray. It's bad for both sides.

Sutra 2.2

You are the reflection of the True Light. Don't allow it to become smudged or obscure it. Let it shine brightly, so that others can clearly see the Path plainly and delight in its beauty.

Chapter Twelve

"Do not think that I have come to abolish the Law or the Prophets; I have come not to abolish but to fulfill. For truly I tell you, until heaven and earth pass away, not one letter, not one stroke of a letter, will pass from the law until all is accomplished.

Therefore, whoever breaks one of the least of these commandments and teaches others to do the same will be called least in the kingdom of heaven, but whoever does them and teaches them will be called great in the kingdom of heaven. For I tell you, unless your righteousness exceeds that of the scribes and Pharisees, you will never enter the kingdom of heaven.[38]"

If you're anything like me, you've heard this line a million times to endorse the doctrine of the Bible's ultimate authority and inerrancy. I remember a pastor explaining "one letter (or) one stroke..." meaning the "jot or tittle" found in the Hebrew alphabet. It's likely this Hebrew concept is what the passage refers to, but not in a proofreading kind of way.

To start, what do we make of this first part: "the Law or the Prophets" Surely, it's not meant to point simply at the covenant God made with Abraham and Moses, followed by the warnings of the Old Testament prophets, therefore Jesus wants us to obey every single word in the Bible (or fraction and structure of the word, if taken literally). Is it? Nope. That way of thinking sells it way too short (believe it or not), and it leads things in the wrong direction.

---

[38] Matthew 5:17-20

The word "law" in Greek is *nomos* (νομος), meaning "to lay down" something, like setting an order for things. The idea isn't so much a list of dos and don'ts, but rather the establishing of how things work in nature, whether at the atomic, environmental, or cosmic[39] scale. Natural law is primary. Man-made laws are lacking at best. We see this theme throughout scripture, from the creation stories, to God's interactions with individuals, with tribes, to many of the Psalms, and what do ya know: to the teachings of Jesus. It continually urges us to recognize what governs every little aspect of life. No need to overcomplicate it.

The word "prophet" in Greek is *prophetes* (προφητης), meaning one who "speaks for" something or someone. In this case, a prophet was one who advocated the ways of the Lord to help society settle into the freedom natural law provides. (Why did we ever feel the need to make prophets into holy fortunetellers or soothsayers?)

By contrast at the time, a Fetial was a priest selected by elites to manipulate the gods by offerings and flattery, thereby

---

[39] Another great place to read where Jesus unpacks Nature is found right at the beginning of the Gospel of Mary. Both *The Teacher, The Twin, & The Tower* and *Maggie's Gospel* puts it this way:

"Everything that is manifest as physical—that is, what is natural, elemental, 'made' so to say of matter, exists in a way that is entangled with everything else," the Teacher replied. "It's all connected in Reality, and its materiality will be dissolved back into Consciousness eventually. Do you remember when I taught you that 'everything comes from Source and everything returns to it?' It's important that you try to understand this."

Later in the commentary sections, it adds this:

"It also brings in concepts like we find in the Upanishad, as well as in quantum physics, where matter is supposed as a condensing and solidifying of Spirit. In Hindu philosophy, *prakriti* (प्रकृति) refers to the primal matter that gives rise to the material world. It's that all–pervading, underlying, eternal essence that constitutes the universe. Saying 77 of *Thom's Gospel* also hints at Spirit underlying all material reality, 'Chop and split a chunk of wood, and you will see that I have embodied it. Look to see what's hiding under a rock, and I am there, too.'"

helping them accept the "terribly constricting conventions of humanity." Let's be honest, they were only there to serve the local government and their own "profits." We'll come back to this later.

So, we have the statement that Jesus is not here to tear down the law of nature that God set in order and harmony, nor to replace those wonderful emissaries, human "angels" who spoke to society in alignment with God's ways.

Next, what does it mean for "heaven and earth" to be completed or transpired? Believe it or not, we can tie this little ditty back to professional fishing from earlier, and it's juxtaposed with another major metaphor: agriculture.

You see, *heaven*, or *ouranos* (ουρανος), derives from the waters, originally meaning "place of rain," but it also extends to all kinds of wetness. It includes what we need to drink and sustain life, what we use to cleanse, brew, baptize with, and well beyond to rivers and to ocean currents, from which creation began and land rose up.

It could even relate to where we draw fish–or wisdom–from.

Then there's *earth*, or *ge* (γη), the "land" we just spoke of, the fertile place of nutrients from which we plant, cultivate, and harvest. It relates to anywhere growth happens, not unlike–should we say–one's heart or mind? Yup. Not unlike that.

So, we've had Fire, Water, Earth... Now all we need is Air. And what do ya bet Jesus brings up next concerning this Law of Nature? It's none other than vowels and consonants, which find their home where? In the air. (Of course!)

Here's the deal: God breathed Life into all of it, and right there in the space between heaven, earth, and ocean is all God, too.

The next part begs the question, doesn't it: Well? What exactly does one do to break these commandments or teach others to break them that would lead one to be called "the least in the kingdom?" No one wants to be on the bottom rung of any kingdom.

The commandments Jesus speaks of go back to how God structured what is natural, right? Compare this with man-made so-called "order", like the Tower of Babel's attempt, or the Israelites' demand of, "Hey, Samuel, get God to give us a king like other nations have." Empires like Rome, or religious groups posturing for more power, exemplify this. It simply doesn't resonate with what God laid down. And so that's how it rightfully earns last place. "Dishonorable mention," if that's a thing.

On the other hand, if one follows the flow of God's laws of nature, they will find themselves in God's very company. No other place like it.

Sutra 2.3

Understand that the teaching speaks to the Law of Nature, not the laws made by human thought. It points to the completeness and wholeness of Source, its Energy, and the All. Anything synthetic or imagined by the mind is a deviation. When such misdirection is taught, it becomes a stagnant, lifeless fragment of True Reality. Yet one who lives in harmony with the Way is wholly One.

Chapter Thirteen

But having a bit of order in society or church isn't all bad, right? Right. In fact, Jesus also addresses some of these structured boundaries and agreements.

The next consecutive passage from the Sermon on the Mount is about anger, which fits nicely with retaliation and love for enemies that come up shortly. But let's just bump the next section down a seat or two so we can talk about this next one.

For now, let's continue with adultery, divorce, and oaths, shall we?

> "You have heard that it was said, 'You shall not commit adultery.' But I say to you that everyone who looks at a woman with lust has already committed adultery with her in his heart. If your right eye causes you to sin, tear it out and throw it away; it is better for you to lose one of your members than for your whole body to be thrown into hell. And if your right hand causes you to sin, cut it off and throw it away; it is better for you to lose one of your members than for your whole body to go into hell."[40]

Here we go again with the "sin and hell" bits. But we cleared that up, remember? It's saying that if something tricks you or trips you up, take the distraction (not the actual person, that would be murder; that's bad,) and throw it far away. Get rid of it, incinerate it, and bury it.

If one is obsessively thinking about someone–sexually stated here, but it could be in any way, really–it has the same effect

---

[40] Matthew 5:27-30

on one's heart. What it's doing is directing their desire upon their will. You see, a divided heart itself is the adultery which violates the very nature and order of the Divine.

WHAT? Who doesn't get distracted in thought? And this sounds serious!

It's said that pain is inevitable, but suffering is optional. In the same way, thoughts arise inevitably, but dwelling on one is a choice. The longer it sits there, the more it bakes on, and the harder it gets to scrape off. Jesus is again making the point that when something adulterates an otherwise pure disposition, that object (or the subject) is not only corrupted, but the contamination spreads. This is the thing that keeps itself from being able to share company with the Divine.

The solution is to be of one heart and mind. It can be hard work. Buddhism addresses this in their Four Noble Truths. Lama Surya Das summarizes them as follows:

1. *Life is difficult.*
2. *Life is difficult because of attachment, because we crave satisfaction in ways that are inherently dissatisfying.*
3. *The possibility of liberation from difficulties exists for everyone.*
4. *The way to realize this liberation and enlightenment is by leading a compassionate life of virtue, wisdom, and meditation. These three spiritual trainings comprise the teachings of the Eightfold Path to Enlightenment.*

The Eightfold Path may take us just a bit further from the purpose here, but one can see the progression it takes:

1. *Right view: Understanding the nature of reality, including the Four Noble Truths.*

2. *Right intention: Avoiding harmful thoughts and cultivating kindness.*
3. *Right speech: Avoiding lies, gossip, and harsh speech; speaking truthfully and kindly.*
4. *Right action: Avoiding harmful actions like killing, stealing, and sexual misconduct.*
5. *Right livelihood: Avoiding trades that harm others and making a living that doesn't exploit others.*
6. *Right effort: Developing a positive state of mind, free from craving and hatred.*
7. *Right mindfulness: Developing awareness of the body, mind, and reality.*
8. *Right concentration: Developing mental focus for meditation.*

The Hindu word for this clinging and craving that comes from letting a thought or feeling linger is *Upādāna* (उपादान), which literally means "fuel." What a perfect way to describe what happens, and why we need to detach from early on before the spark of a thought gets out of hand, and *BOOM!* What a mess we've made!

Sutra 3.1

You've been told your whole life that doing something bad is wrong. But even allowing it to linger as a thought is harmful, because this is where it contaminates the heart and poisons the soul. Detach yourself from the very notion, and it won't fester into desire.

Chapter Fourteen

This topic of adultery and now divorce seems to touch its social construct like divorce, and for more apologetic reasons rather than its strictly historical accuracy. At least, I'm chalking this up to that. But even so, there's something worth gleaning here.

> "It was also said, 'Whoever divorces his wife, let him give her a certificate of divorce.' But I say to you that anyone who divorces his wife, except on the grounds of sexual immorality, causes her to commit adultery, and whoever marries a divorced woman commits adultery.[41]"

To get what I'm saying, a bit of background might help. First, it was ridiculously easy for a man to divorce a woman over the pettiest reasons at the time. Does anyone else find it interesting that it dismisses wives divorcing husbands, or do we expect it from our patriarchal authors? Not so fast, the same scene seems to happen also in Mark's Gospel, and Jewish law did provide grounds where women could have cause for divorce.[42]

Even Jesus, when confronted by Pharisees who were trying to trap him over divorce by citing Deuteronomic law, offers a better way:

---

[41] Matthew 5:31-32

[42] Shown in Mark 10:1-12, coming up. And if you're a stickler over this, I'd invite you to check out *Ketubot* 39 (...When she initiates the divorce, he can divorce her), *Mishnah Kiddushin* 1 (And a woman acquires for herself a bill of divorce...), *Mishnah Gittin* 2 (Additionally, a woman can write her own bill of divorce and give it to her husband so that he can present it to her), and in *Bava Batra* 168 (The Gemara adds: But today, the reason that we do not do so, but instead have the woman pay the scribe, is that the Sages placed the burden upon the woman, so that the husband should not delay the divorce by refusing to pay the scribe.) Yes, the Mishnah was written after the earliest version of the gospels, but the rabbinic practices and legal precedence was already established.

"He left that place and went to the region of Judea and beyond the Jordan. Crowds gathered around him again, and as was his custom, he taught them.

"Some, testing him, asked, 'Is it lawful for a man to divorce his wife?'

"He answered, 'What did Moses command you?'

"They said, 'Moses allowed a man to write a certificate of dismissal and to divorce her.'

"But Jesus said, 'Because of your hardness of heart, he wrote this commandment for you. But from the beginning of creation, God made them male and female. For this reason, a man shall leave his father and mother and be joined to his wife, and the two shall become one flesh. So, they are no longer two but one flesh. Therefore, what God has joined together, let no one separate.'

"Then in the house, the disciples asked him again about this matter.

"He said to them, 'Whoever divorces his wife and marries another commits adultery against her, **and if she divorces her husband and marries another, she commits adultery**.[43]'"

So, there you have it. But aside from that, why would Jesus even bring up divorce in the Sermon on the Mount? It's worth noting that this comes at a time when Herodias had just divorced Philip to marry his brother Herod Antipas, aka King Herod, and it had been making headlines. Divorce was trending hard.

---

[43] Mark 10:3-12

The thing about divorce in those days (like sometimes today) was that it had become more about shirking the responsibility and concern for one's family. It was about selfishly disregarding others, especially the partner you've united yourself with.

That's the underlying teaching here as well, beyond the sacrament, sacredness of marriage, or social arrangement. Divorce, like adultery, can be viewed on many levels. Jesus confronts us with where our heart truly belongs. Are you bound to ignorance? Married, as it were, to doctrines or beliefs that don't align with your True Self? Is your commitment really to your own self-centered ways and to chasing desires, away from God or family?

Jesus presents another clever twist, calling one out to "go public" with how they identify and to their commitment to community and Path.

Addressing the deeper issues of adultery and divorce is important enough that he returns to the principle a bit later, you'll soon see it with "serving two masters."

Notice also how the topic of divorce follows the earlier teaching about contamination of the heart, and flows naturally into making oaths next. Its meaning is subtle, but definitely connects to something more than being extra conservative with our contracts.

Sutra 3.2

Let go of your old ways. Show that you mean it. Commit to the Path for-fully, not more toying with the past or dragging it along. Make the break and don't look back.

Chapter Fifteen

"Again, you have heard that it was said to those of ancient times, 'You shall not swear falsely, but carry out the vows you have made to the Lord.' But I say to you: Do not swear at all, either by heaven, for it is the throne of God, or by the earth, for it is his footstool, or by Jerusalem, for it is the city of the great King. And do not swear by your head, for you cannot make one hair white or black. Let your word be 'Yes, or 'No; anything more than this comes from the evil one.[44]"

Here we find another example of the phrase, "you've heard it said like this, but I say that." Some folks will debate that this shows Jesus had close ties to the Pharisees. After all, wasn't he often in their company, in homes, on rooftops, where they gathered? Didn't he share several ideas and familiarity with Scripture? Wasn't he always trying to get to Jerusalem, the religious "headquarters" of Judaism? Sure. But historically, Pharisees weren't really present in Galilee, where he grew up, until much later. And there were other teachers like John the Baptist or Hillel the Elder, who also would have influenced his religious thought and spiritual formation at the time.

The phrase is likely as much a rhetorical style[45] of speech as anything, but one that carries real substance.

---

[44] Matthew 5:33-37

[45] Consider also this style and look at how John the Baptist puts this from Luke 3:10-14: And the crowds asked him, "What, then, should we do?" In reply he said to them, "Whoever has two coats must share with anyone who has none, and whoever has food must do likewise." Even tax collectors came to be baptized, and they asked him, "Teacher, what should we do?" He said to them, "Collect no more than the amount prescribed for you." Soldiers also asked him, "And we, what should we do?" He said to them, "Do not extort money from anyone by threats or false accusation, and be satisfied with your wages."

This substance echoes throughout Stoicism, too, teaching that integrity plays a major role in being virtuous and fully human. It stresses the importance of consistency in actions and character. Stoics were known for living according to their own values, even under pressure to do otherwise.

There are some other Stoic traits that sound right up Jesus' alley,[46] such as:

- *Be a witness to yourself; don't seek approval from others but focus on your own integrity.*
- *Be consistent, reliable, and trustworthy by showing the same virtues in all situations.*
- *Don't accept social, political, or religious dogma without challenging and questioning it for yourself.*
- *Do the right thing, period. "Waste no time arguing about what a good man should be. Be one."*

-Marcus Aurelius.

This is exactly what Jesus is getting at here. First, he warned us about what pulls us off the right path, then about letting go of old thoughts and habits and shifting direction. Now he's telling us how to move forward in that new direction.

---

[46] Let's talk a bit about Jesus' alley. And when I say his alley, I mean a lot of folks' alleys. We tend to think—because we've been told—Jesus was a Jew; therefore, he followed Judaism. However, there were many schools of thought, even within Judaism back in 30 CE (Pharisees, Sadducees, Essences, Zealots, Nazarenes, Herodians, Sicarii, etc.). Not only Stoicism, but Cynicism and Platonism were also big influences on the Jewish philosophy of the time, as seen with Philo, and later on early Christianity with the likes of Clement, Origen, the Cappadocian Fathers, Augstine, and so on. By the time the Middle Ages and Renaissance came along, the church had adopted much from Platonism. We see it even today.

Sutra 3.3

Be wise. Be brave. Let go of making promises, whether you keep them or not. It's better to simply walk with integrity, not to impress, not to perform. Speak from the heart, where lip service has no place.

Chapter Sixteen

We're going to keep shifting the topics around just a bit. The different gospels do all the time—changing up the order of when things were said—so we're in good company. Here, his focus remains unchanged: it's still about the heart, but Jesus now turns his attention to a few religious rites and practices.

His teachings on oaths flow naturally into his thoughts on charity, fasting, and prayer:

> "Beware of practicing your righteousness before others in order to be seen by them, for then you have no reward from your Father in heaven.

> "So, whenever you give alms, do not sound a trumpet before you, as the hypocrites do in the synagogues and in the streets, so that they may be praised by others. Truly I tell you, they have received their reward. But when you give alms, do not let your left hand know what your right hand is doing, so that your alms may be done in secret, and your Father who sees in secret will reward you.[47]"

Once again, Jesus places virtue above legalism. He's shown us how easy it is to get caught up in distractions and empty habits. What we need is a bit of a course correction, but not toward more ritual for ritual's sake, and certainly not by pretending to be something we're not. Performance Christianity is just pride in disguise, and it's disgusting. It not only gets in the way of seeing the Divine in others and elevating those in need, but it also flips the entire thing on its head. It becomes self-elevating, missing the point entirely.

---

[47] Matthew 6:1-4

Hands that cling to what they have, often in overabundance, aren't empty. Fists are made from clutching one's grip. Yet empty hands are open and able to receive anything from the Divine. They can also take the hands of someone reaching out for help.

To be totally honest, I think the author of Matthew's Gospel may have offered a somewhat shallow interpretation here. I do not think the teaching was only "don't be showy about giving, because the compliments are all you're gonna get from it, but if you do it in secret then God will reward you with a much higher return on investments." That's a punishment-reward framing that still centers on the self.

To me, the version of this teaching found in the Gospel of Thomas offers a deeper take.

> Jesus said, "Two will rest on a couch. One will die, the other will live."
>
> Salome said, "Who are you, Sir, to climb onto my couch and eat off my table as if you're from someone?"
>
> Jesus said to her, "I'm the one who exists in equality. Some of what belongs to my Father was given to me."
>
> "I'm your disciple." (said Salome,) "So I'm telling you, if someone is equal, they'll be full of light; but if they're divided, they'll be full of darkness."
>
> Jesus said, "I tell my mysteries to those who are worthy of my mysteries. Don't let your left hand know what your right hand is doing."

A rephrasing puts it this way (from *Thom's Gospel*):

> "I'm happy to explain these deeper things, but only with those who know their value. Here's what I mean:

your left and right hands don't need to explain themselves to one another in order to understand."

I believe the idea that Jesus was getting at is that in true equality, the left and right hands both extend from the same heart, flowing outward from the same Oneness.

"Don't let the left hand know what your right hand is doing" doesn't imply secrecy out of suspicion or shame. It implies unity. Just like Salome affirmed that she was equally full of Light. Even when our hands aren't engaged in the same task at the same time, each one still shines with the same vibrancy from the same Consciousness.

(Side note: we'll skip the next section on prayer for now, since it gets a chapter of its own.)

The same idea applies to fasting:[48]

> "And whenever you fast, do not look somber, like the hypocrites, for they mark their faces to show others that they are fasting.
>
> Truly I tell you, they have received their reward.
>
> But when you fast, put oil on your head and wash your face, so that your fasting may not be seen by others but by your Father who is in secret; and your Father who sees in secret will reward you."

Again, I don't think we should reduce the teaching to a transactional "do this in secret and God will pay you back." That reading—in common with Matthew—sells it short, like I said. The teaching isn't about hiding your good deeds to gain

---

[48] Matthew 6:16-18

spiritual bonus points. It's about realigning our motivations entirely.

The Gospel of Thomas–which likely predates the canonized gospels– ties all of these practices together (fasting, prayer, charity, dietary restrictions) and presents them beautifully:

> His disciples said to him, "Do you want us to fast? And how should we pray? Should we make donations? And what food should we avoid?"
>
> Jesus said, "Don't lie, and don't do what you hate, because everything is revealed in the sight of heaven; for there's nothing hidden that won't be revealed, and nothing covered up that will stay secret.[49]"

And… a special diet too? I'd be out, no doubt!

Thankfully, Jesus doesn't exclude anyone on that basis either. (*Whew.*)

Do you see how this flows naturally from the previous teachings about keeping oaths? If so, you'll appreciate how Jesus keeps weaving the same golden thread of inner clarity, honesty, and Oneness through every teaching that follows.

Jesus isn't rejecting prayer, fasting, or giving altogether. He's pointing us back to the heart of the matter. He's calling us to practice these things not for recognition, but from a place of inner integrity, a heart centered in compassion, equality, and awareness.

---

[49] Gospel of Thomas, Saying 6. And the verse before it also ties in nicely to all of this, too:

Saying 5 says, "Know what's in front of your face, and what's hidden from you will be revealed to you, because there's nothing hidden that won't be revealed." Of course, he repeats this quite a bit, and just like what we saw from Sayings 61 & 62. So, it seems like a tricky teaching, at least for his disciples. But I'm sure it's not so bad for us, right? (*Wink!*)

Sutra 3.4

Remember that spiritual practices can easily become performances. So when you engage in them, let it be with the understanding that they are meant to cultivate balance and equality, to deepen your recognition of Oneness.

Chapter Seventeen

I said we'd come back to the part we skipped on prayer, so here it is.

The Lord's Prayer, like the Beatitudes, comes straight out of the Sermon on the Mount. We find its most familiar version in the Gospel of Matthew, though Luke's Sermon on the Plain includes a shorter version, and the *Didache* offers a slightly longer one (and has that last line which we are familiar with from the song; I grew up singing it in church and didn't know it wasn't in my Bible for a long, long time).

Just like with giving to charity, the emphasis here is clear: don't turn prayer into a production. Let's be honest, showing off through a prayer isn't impressive. It's performative spirituality at best, and at worst, it turns sacred space into ego theatrics.

The guidance Jesus gives is to pray in private. Not because prayer itself should be hidden or ashamed of, but because intimacy with the Divine is easily distracted by the eyes and opinions of others. The point is to cultivate a real connection with Oneness, not to impress people. And because Consciousness already "knows" what's going on, there's no need to get overly wordy, mantric, or rigid in our focus. The invitation is to welcome us into real alignment, not repetition.

In other words, he says our prayers might sound something more like this:[50]

---

[50] From Matthew 6:5-15, shown in parentheses

Sutra 4.1

("Our Father in heaven, may your name be revered as holy.")

> *We recognize the Divine as the Source from which we are manifested and in which we are continually cultivated. It is Consciousness that imbues all things, not just here, but beyond, and everywhere.*

Sutra 4.2

("May your kingdom come. May your will be done, on earth as in heaven.")

> *May it unveil the realization of True Reality, penetrating us, and pervading through us. As it already is, beyond form and illusion.*

Sutra 4.3

("Give us today our daily bread.")

> *This Pure Awareness sustains us, on every plane, in every form.*

Sutra 4.4

("And forgive us our debts, as we also have forgiven our debtors.")

> *It restores us to our True Self from ignorance, as we, in turn, extend grace and patience to others.*

Sutra 4.5

("And do not bring us to the time of trial, but rescue us from the evil one.")

> *May the Light of Consciousness shine in us and through us so purely that distractions and illusions hold no sway.*

(The Didache adds: "For yours is the power and the glory forever and ever.")

Toto Tay

Now, Make It Yours

As I was writing, I asked my friend Sandy what her thoughts were on this. She said she liked it and that she actually uses her own "alternative" version of the Lord's Prayer!

That reminded me I had done something similar, long ago, when my now-adult kids were just toddlers. I'd be holding them, rocking back and forth, trying to get them to sleep. Sometimes I'd feel drawn to pray, but pray *what*? I didn't want to just spiral into all the worries and fears every parent faces. And I needed something that wasn't rote, but *mine*.

So, I sat down and scribbled something out, something just for that moment. It went a little like this:

O, Divine One!

I ask that You would guide me
In being more like You,
In kindness, in compassion,
Patience and forgiveness.

As You are wise, help me to think
Before I speak, before I act,
To be mindfully aware
And deeply observant.

Be my ever-present shield
From infections, allergens, toxins.
Protect me from harmful energies,
And from negative thoughts.
Fill my mind with peace, my heart with joy,

73

And my hands and feet with strength,
That I may share and care as You do,
For all of Your creation. (Including me!)
So be it.

Really, Toto? *Infections? Allergens?* That was your big concern?

Yup. Some of it. That's just where I was at the time, as a new parent and a bit of a health nut. I'll admit I'm in a slightly different place now, both in terms of my relaxed germaphobia and my metaphysical understanding. But I can tell you that simple little prayer helped me *immensely*.

Interestingly, I just found out that another good friend, Jim, did something similar, as I was working on this. He was given the prompt, "Write a letter to Jesus," and I was amazed at how beautifully in sync his words were. Here's what he wrote:

Divine One

Grant me the balance to be present to your Spirit.
Grant that my heart may be carefully open.
Be the buffer I need to let the struggles of the world pass through me without sticking.
Reduce my need for attachment.
May the lovingkindness of your Mother at the cradle,
And the pierced heart of the tears you shed for Lazarus,
Be reflected out of me
As the grace of your active love in the world.
May it not be me who is seen,
But the image of You, Yourself.

Toto Tay

Rewriting or reframing "The Lord's Prayer" is also a wonderful contemplative practice. Why not give it a whirl and see what comes up for you!

Chapter Eighteen

Well, that was fun. But remember that other bit we skipped? Just after Jesus "laid down the Law"? Here it is, now:

> "You have heard that it was said to those of ancient times, 'You shall not murder,' and 'whoever murders shall be liable to judgment.'
>
> But I say to you that if you are angry with a brother or sister, you will be liable to judgment; and if you insult a brother or sister, you will be liable to the council; and if you say, 'You fool,' you will be liable to the hell of fire.
>
> So, when you are offering your gift at the altar, if you remember that your brother or sister has something against you, leave your gift there before the altar and go; first be reconciled to your brother or sister, and then come and offer your gift.
>
> Come to terms quickly with your accuser while you are on the way to court with him, or your accuser may hand you over to the judge, and the judge to the guard, and you will be thrown into prison. Truly I tell you, you will never get out until you have paid the last penny.[51]"

Huh?

Without getting completely sidetracked by parsing the difference between calling someone *Raca* versus "fool" (*moros*, yep, like *moron*), maybe it's still worth a brief chase. Then we'll go back to the main point.

---

[51] Matthew 5:21-26

Let's break it down in basic terms. It's the difference between a run-of-the-mill insult and something with deeper implications. The Greek word *moros* has been linked (somewhat weirdly) to the idea of "mulberry juice." And yes, mulberry juice does stain badly. But that alone doesn't really clarify things yet. So, let's keep going.

"Raca" might be the equivalent of calling someone a "blockhead" or "dummy." It's an insult, sure, but not a deeply spiritual accusation. *Moros,* however, carries a sharper edge. It suggests calling someone hollow, essentially, hastily accusing them of not having the "right stuff" or substance inside (without really understanding if they do or not). In other words, it's a rash judgment of someone's essence rather than just their behavior, a reactionary *ad hominem*. And that kind of projection can land you, spiritually speaking, right in the smelly ol' garbage heap, Gehenna (yep, that place again).

So, what's Jesus saying here?

Before you lose your cool with someone, no matter how justified your frustration may seem, and no matter which side of the conflict you're on, tap into some of that self-control that we're meant to be cultivating right about now. Then tack on some grace. Work it out, make peace.

Because, as the saying goes: *karma's a bitch.*

By the way, *Karma Yoga* is one of the three main spiritual paths described in the Bhagavad Gita, alongside *Jnana Yoga* (the path of knowledge) and *Bhakti Yoga* (the path of devotion).

Karma Yoga is the path of action, doing everything as an offering, as service to Krishna, in every aspect of daily life.

Chapter Three of the Bhagavad Gita explores this path extensively. (See Appendix Three for Sanskrit and transliteration.) It says:

> "One cannot achieve freedom from karmic reactions by merely abstaining from work, nor can one attain perfection of knowledge by mere physical renunciation.
>
> There is no one who can remain without action even for a moment. Indeed, all beings are compelled to act by their qualities born of material nature (the three *guṇas*).
>
> Those who restrain the external organs of action, while continuing to dwell on sense objects in the mind, certainly delude themselves and are to be called hypocrites.
>
> But those karma yogis who control their knowledge-senses with the mind, O Arjuna, and engage the working senses in action without attachment, are certainly superior.
>
> You should thus perform your prescribed duties, since action is superior to inaction. Even the maintenance of your body wouldn't be possible without work.
>
> Work must be done as a sacrifice to the Supreme Lord; otherwise, it leads to bondage in this material world. Therefore, O Arjuna, perform your duties for the satisfaction of God, without attachment to the results.
>
> In the beginning of creation, Brahma created humankind along with duties and said:

'Prosper through the performance of these *yajñas* (sacrifices), for they shall bestow upon you all that you wish to achieve.'"

It's wild, right?

In Ayurveda (India's traditional system of medicine), overindulging in dairy can cause diarrhea. And yet, the cure for that same type of digestive upset? A little bit of dairy, specifically yogurt, mixed with boiled rice and a pinch of salt.

The same substance that caused the issue is also the remedy. "We rise by the same ground that trips us," as the Hindu proverb reminds us. (As an aside, this includes approaching nonduality or the Universal Christ; we learn to understand it from wherever we're at, that is, from a dualistic, dogmatic mindset.)

And in the same way, our actions, or *karma*, can either bind us to the material world or liberate us from it, depending on how and *why* they're performed.

So, if we act from ego, judgment, or to be controlling, we stay entangled. But if we act from clarity, compassion, and service, then those very same actions become the path to awakening.

Wild indeed.

Sutra 5.1

When in conflict with another, keep your head in check and move from the heart. Set things right by recognizing the Divine in the other, and know you're doing it also for the Divine.

Chapter Nineteen

Like we've said before, sometimes the Sermon on the Mount feels like it jumps around a bit in its topics. I'm not entirely sure why. But for our purposes here, and for the sake of clarity, it makes sense to arrange the teachings so they glide more smoothly from one to the next. The goal, after all, is just to understand them better. Right?

> "Do not store up for yourselves treasures on earth, where moth and rust consume and where thieves break in and steal.
>
> But store up for yourselves treasures in heaven, where neither moth nor rust consume and where thieves do not break in and steal.
>
> For where your treasure is, there your heart will be also.[52]"

We find a strikingly similar idea at the end of a parable in the Gospel of Thomas, Saying 76. There, Jesus says:

> "The Father's kingdom can be compared to a merchant with merchandise who found a pearl.
>
> The merchant was wise; they sold their merchandise and bought that single pearl for themselves.
>
> You, too, look for the treasure that doesn't perish but endures, where no moths come to eat and no worms destroy."

I don't know whether Matthew borrowed this from Thomas (as some scholars believe, and I tend to lean in that direction), or

---

[52] Matthew 5:19-21

maybe it's just such a great line that Jesus repeated it on several occasions. Either way, it resonates deeply.

We also see a similar theme echoed in the Gospel of Mary, in the surviving fragments from page 10:

> "Lord, I saw you in a vision today…"
>
> In response, he said to me, "You're blessed because you didn't waver at the sight of me. For where the mind is, there is the treasure."

Wait, did that say *mind* instead of *heart*? It sure did.

Do you remember back in Chapter Two, when Paul's prayer included the phrase, *"having the eyes of the heart enlightened"*? That's the same "heart" referenced here in Matthew's Gospel. The Greek word used is *kardia* (καρδία), and it doesn't just refer to the physical organ in your chest; it often points to one's *mental disposition* or *interior orientation*.

Now, the Coptic text of the Gospel of Mary uses the word *nous* (ⲚⲞⲨⲤ), meaning *mind, intelligence,* or even *intuition*. In a way, this "organ" is a kind of bridge. In *Maggie's Gospel*, I rendered it like this:

> "It's wonderful you can realize that the Awareness rises up here in the heartmind,[53] where Humanity and Divinity intertwine."

So, are we seeing the authors of these gospels swapping notes? Or is this just one of those brilliant, crowd-pleasing lines Jesus repeated often?

---

[53] - In Chinese philosophy, the concept of *xin* (心) combines both the heart and mind, literally "heartmind." It's the idea that understanding, intention, and one's feeling about something are all from one space. Emotions without intellect or using reason without reading the mood is a sign of an undeveloped or fragmented cognition.

Honestly? DKDC (Don't Know, Don't Care). Either way, it's fantastic and worth paying attention to.

Because the "treasure" being talked about here, that which can only truly be perceived with the heartmind, is better than gold.

Interestingly, the Greek word for "treasure" in Matthew is *thēsauros* (θησαυρός). Yep, like thesaurus. A storehouse of riches. Or in this case, the storehouse of what's gathered from the All.

And just like when Paul writes to his friends in Colossae and Laodicea (emphasis mine):

> "I want your hearts to be encouraged and united in love, so that you may have all the *riches* of assured understanding and have the *knowledge* of God's *mystery*, that is, Christ, in whom are hidden *all the treasures of wisdom and knowledge.*[54] "

And that's really something.

Sutra 5.2

Don't be distracted by fleeting thoughts or temporal goals. Instead, let your heartmind perceive where true value lies, and give your full attention to that.

---

[54] Colossian 2:2-3

Chapter Twenty

Both the Sermon on the Mount and the Sermon on the Plain offer this central teaching about loving your enemies and the Golden Rule.

Several other religious traditions have similar teachings, many of which even precede Jesus.

Take *The Eloquent Peasant*, an ancient Egyptian tale from the 19th century BCE. It contains this line:

> "Do for one who may do for you, that you may cause him thus to do."

The Upanishads, written between 800–600 BCE, offer this:

> "Let no man do to another that which would be repugnant to himself; this is the sum of righteousness; the rest is according to inclination. In refusing, in bestowing, in regard to pleasure and to pain, to what is agreeable and disagreeable, a man obtains the proper rule by regarding the case as like his own."

Around 400 BCE, the Greek thinker Isocrates wrote:

> "Do not do to others that which angers you when they do it to you."

The Bhagavad Gita, written around the same era, gives us this beautiful verse:

> "I regard them to be perfect yogis who see the true equality of all living beings and respond to the joys and sorrows of others as if they were their own." (6.32)

And then there's Rabbi Hillel, whose teaching is famously aligned with (and likely had a strong influence on) Jesus:

"That which is hateful to you, do not do to your neighbor: that is the whole of the Torah, while the rest is commentary thereon; go and learn it."

Zoroastrians, Buddhists, Taoists, and Muslims all have their own versions,[55] too.

So, if there's a universal "top ten list" of spiritual truths, the Golden Rule is absolutely on it.

Now that we know where we're heading, let's take a closer look at Jesus' teaching, as recorded in Luke:

"But I say to you who are listening: Love your enemies; do good to those who hate you; bless those who curse you; pray for those who mistreat you.

If anyone strikes you on the cheek, offer the other also; and from anyone who takes away your coat, do not withhold even your shirt.

Give to everyone who asks of you, and if anyone takes away what is yours, do not ask for it back again.

Do to others as you would have them do to you.

If you love those who love you, what credit is that to you? For even sinners love those who love them.

If you do good to those who do good to you, what credit is that to you? Even sinners do the same.

---

[55] There's a lot of scholarly works about this, including several from the late 19th and early 20th century. But here's a more recent one I really liked:

Bakker, Freek. (2012). *Comparing the Golden Rule in Hindu and Christian Religious Texts.* Studies in Religion/Sciences Religieuses. 42. 38-58. DOI: 10.1177/0008429812460141.

If you lend to those from whom you expect to receive, what credit is that to you? Even sinners lend to sinners, expecting to be repaid in full.

Instead, love your enemies, do good, and lend, expecting nothing in return. Then your reward will be great, and you will be children of the Highest, for he himself is kind to the ungrateful and the wicked.[56]

"Be merciful, just as your Father is merciful."

This comes from Luke's version in the Sermon on the Plain. Oh yeah, that bit about mercy is nixed and nowhere to be found from Matthew's account. In its place we read,

"Be perfect, therefore, as your heavenly Father is perfect.[57]"

Matthew also begins the section with a rhetorical setup:

"You have heard that it was said, 'An eye for an eye and a tooth for a tooth.' But I say to you: Do not resist an evildoer...[58]"

Now, I don't want to wander too far from Luke's version, but this part in Matthew needs some explanation.

First, not only does Matthew skip the mercy, but he also gives us a phrase that's been, unfortunately, mistranslated. Nearly all English versions say "evildoer," "evil person," or "one who is evil." But the Greek word used here is *ponēros* (πονηρός),

---

[56] Luke 6:27-36. The same bit from Matthew starts in chapter 5, verses 43-48, and adds "The Golden Rule" closer to the end, in chapter 7, verse 12.

[57] Matthew 5:48

[58] Matthew 5:39

which refers more to something subjected to pain, suffering, distress, or disgrace.

By saying that we shouldn't resist "evil done to us" takes it in a weird direction. I strongly believe Jesus means something different. Being struck, sued, forced to carry a Roman soldier's equipment, treated indignantly, cursed at, or whatever, is how the slaves, the outcast and abandoned, the "less than human" were treated every day. This would mean that we are not to fight back against evil in the violent sense, but when we accept when we're subjected to disgrace or hardship, it's not the last word. In fact, Christ suffers alongside us and uses it to show us the bigger picture and to grow us into something majestic.

Now, let me be clear: "Be perfect" has its place. But not in the guilt-ridden, sin-obsessed, unattainable way we often interpret it. And it's certainly not meant as the bait-and-switch narrative where the "Father God took sinless Jesus, our unblemished Lamb, and swapped spilling our blood for his, which covers us like Carrie at prom, so that the Father (who demands absolute 'perfection') looks at us and only sees the tissue of his flawless son, so I guess that means we're *perfect*," either.

The word there is *teleios* (τελειος), and it means being whole and fully complete, like how the entire full-grown, fruit-bearing tree is contained within the tiny seed. Even though it may feel like it's shoved into the depths of darkness and crushed by the weight of the soil, just wait. That seed is going to grow roots and rise into something majestic.

Still, if I had to choose, I would much prefer Luke's *mercy* over Matthew's *perfection*.

But once you understand what both actually mean, they work together beautifully.

And remember back in the Beatitudes and Sutra 1.5?

"Blessed are the merciful" (ἐλεήμονες, *eleēmones*), those who fill in the gap of what another lacks in order to follow the will of society (or God).

This fits so well with the dynamic flow of love between God, us, and each other.

Sutra 6.1

When someone treats you like a nobody, demonstrate that you see others equally, by choosing to love and serve. Isn't this how the Divine treats us? And in return for such generosity, we receive the gift of recognizing how Ultimate Reality operates.

Chapter Twenty-One

Closely related, and also found in both the Sermon on the Mount and the Sermon on the Plain, is the teaching on judging others. Honestly, I prefer Luke's account here, too. It feels more substantial, and it tightly weaves the concept of judgment with forgiveness, which really gets to the heart of the matter. Matthew's version comes off a bit more "judgy" (uh oh, am I judging Matthew too harshly?).

> "Do not judge, and you will not be judged; do not condemn, and you will not be condemned. Forgive, and you will be forgiven; give, and it will be given to you. A good measure, pressed down, shaken together, running over, will be put into your lap, for the measure you give will be the measure you get back."

Then Jesus told them a parable:

> "Can a blind person guide a blind person? Will not both fall into a pit? A disciple is not above the teacher, but every disciple who is fully qualified will be like the teacher. Why do you see the speck in your neighbor's eye but do not notice the log in your own eye? Or how can you say to your neighbor, 'Friend, let me take out the speck in your eye,' when you yourself do not see the log in your own eye? You hypocrite, first take the log out of your own eye, and then you will see clearly to take the speck out of your neighbor's eye.[59]"

---

[59] Luke 6:37-42. The parallel text from the Sermon on the Mount from Matthew 7:15 reads: "Do not judge, so that you may not be judged. For the judgment you give will be the judgment you get, and the measure you give will be the measure you get. Why do you see the speck in your neighbor's eye but do not notice the log in your own eye? Or how can you say to your neighbor, 'Let me take the speck out of your eye,' while the log is in your own eye? You

Interestingly, this last paragraph finds parallels in the Gospel of Thomas, sayings 26 and 34.

Sometimes we mean judging as assessing or discerning (this is good). Other times, we mean judging as in criticizing or fault-finding, which can be harmful and condescending. That first part, "don't judge or you'll be judged", sounds a lot like karma yoga, doesn't it? I mean, it's really good stuff, right?

But I don't want us to just breeze past the forgiveness part either. We all know what forgiveness is. It's the harder part a lot of times. Tough to swallow our pride when we're wrong, but also sometimes tough to let go of our pain when we're on the receiving end. From a place of hurt, it's hard to do a lot of things, especially to forgive someone.

This passage seems to say *Justice matters, sure, but more than that, I'm choosing rehabilitation and restoration.*

So, what does this "well-measured, pressed down, shaken up, running over" measure actually mean? It's saying that to the exact degree you let go and empty yourself of condemnation and contempt, you will be filled. Not just filled, but overflowing. Grace, forgiveness, and restoration will be heaped upon you so completely that you'll have to hold out your shirt just to catch it all, and even then it will spill all over! The seed of forgiveness yields a hundredfold harvest.

Jesus then urges them to pay attention because their focus is off, it's on the wrong things, and that distraction puts them in danger of stumbling.

---

hypocrite, first take the log out of your own eye, and then you will see clearly to take the speck out of your neighbor's eye."

See? Nothing about forgiveness, no "blind leading the blind" bit, just kind of "judgy."

He models the humility he's talking about with the line, "A disciple is not above the teacher, but every disciple who is fully qualified will be like the teacher." What we see is that there is equality here. The speck in someone's eye is so close that from their perspective, it looks like a log. When that's out of the way and one truly perceives with clarity and empathy, what do they see but the Divine reflected back? Amirite?

Sutra 6.2

Stop condemning. Stop criticizing. It clouds the heart and obscures what matters most. Forgive, and release your grip on what's been done to you. Then you will be filled, overflowing, restored, and healed. If you clean your heart's eyes of this obstruction, then you'll behold the world's vibrant beauty once again.

Chapter Twenty-Two

Don't judge. Got it. Forgive. You betcha. But don't toss out all of the ways that we judge things. Huh?

Yeah, remember when we said there's bad judging, but there's also good judging? This is what we call discernment.

Both Luke and Matthew include this next part in their respective sermons. Just for fun, let's look at them side by side. As we've come to expect, there's a slight difference.[60] Luke continues with this:

> "No good tree bears bad fruit, nor again does a bad tree bear good fruit; for each tree is known by its own fruit. For people do not gather figs from thorns, nor do they pick grapes from a bramble bush. The good person out of the good treasure of the heart produces good, and the evil person out of evil treasure produces evil, for it is out of the abundance of the heart that the mouth speaks."

Matthew's account goes:

> "Beware of false prophets, who come to you in sheep's clothing but inwardly are ravenous wolves. You will know them by their fruits. Are grapes gathered from thorns or figs from thistles? In the same way, every good tree bears good fruit, but the bad tree bears bad fruit. A good tree cannot bear bad fruit, nor can a bad tree bear good fruit. Every tree that does not bear good fruit will be cut down and thrown into the fire. Thus, you will know them by their fruits."

---

[60] Luke 6:42-45 followed by Matthew 7:15-20, a few verses later

So, what's with all the theatrics? Matthew charges right in with: "Beware! False prophets! Looking like sweet little baby lambs, but really ravenous wolves! Grrrowl!" And no less dramatic, he finishes on this rather violent note: "If you don't produce tasty fruit, I'm gonna take a rusty ax to ya and chuck you into the blazing fire! Hahaha!!!"

Let's ask Thomas what he thinks Jesus said. Here's Saying 45:

> "Grapes aren't harvested from thorns, nor are figs gathered from thistles, because they don't produce fruit. A person who's good brings good things out of their treasure, and a person who is evil brings evil things out of their evil treasure. They say evil things because their heart is full of evil."

Let's stick with how Luke and Thomas tone it down.

There's also a Buddhist text called the Sappurisa Sutta[61] that offers a wise perspective on the right attitude:

> "Now, a person endowed with these four qualities can be known as 'a person of integrity.' Which four?
>
> There is the case where a person of integrity, when asked, does not reveal another person's bad points, not to mention when unasked. Furthermore, when pressed with questions, they speak of another's bad points not in full detail, holding back. Of this person you may know, 'This venerable one is a person of integrity.'
>
> Then, a person of integrity, when unasked, reveals another's good points, to say nothing of when asked. Furthermore, when asked, when pressed with

---

[61] Found in the *Anguttara Nikaya*, (Numerical Discourses) 4.73 (beautifully translated from Pali by Thanissaro Bhikkhu)

questions, he is one who speaks of another person's good points in full and detail, without holding back. You may know, 'This venerable one is a person of integrity.'

A person of integrity, when unasked, reveals their own bad points, and certainly when asked. When pressed with questions, he is one who speaks of his own bad points in full & in detail, without omissions, without holding back. Of this person you may know, 'This venerable one is a person of integrity.'

And finally, a person of integrity, when asked, does not reveal their own good points, not to mention when unasked. When pressed, they speak of their own good points partially, holding back. Of this person you may know, 'This venerable one is a person of integrity.'

"Monks, a person endowed with these four qualities can be known as 'a person of integrity.'"

Honestly, there will always be aspects about people that others should know plainly, but opinions are too often disguised as facts. So, we must not rush to speak out and risk it harming others.

"To pass judgment hurriedly doesn't mean you're a judge. The wise one, weighing both the right judgment & wrong, judges others impartially, unhurriedly, in line with the Dhamma, guarding the Dhamma, guarded by Dhamma, intelligent: he's called a judge.[62]"

The rendering for this next sutra borrows much from the modern translation of *Thom's Gospel* (saying 45).

---

[62] *Dhammapada* 256-257 (also Thanissaro Bhikku)

Sutra 6.3

If kindness, gentleness, compassion, patience, and peace are already growing in your heart, they will naturally overflow into your words and actions. One who speaks or behaves in harmful ways does so because that is what fills them within.

Chapter Twenty-Three

I admit it, I may have been too quick to judge the Sermon on the Mount's take. Matthew can be a bit melodramatic, sure, but his warning about "false prophets" is not without merit. We touched on this theme earlier in Chapter Sixteen (Sutra 3.4) and how one's fasting, praying, and giving to charity can be hypocritically misleading.

The following teaching from Matthew's account is this:

> "Not everyone who says to me, 'Lord, Lord,' will enter the kingdom of heaven, but only the one who does the will of my Father in heaven. On that day many will say to me, 'Lord, Lord, did we not prophesy in your name, and cast out demons in your name, and do many mighty works in your name?' Then I will declare to them, 'I never knew you; go away from me, you who behave lawlessly.[63]'"

If that sounds familiar, it's because it echoes the parable of the sheep and the goats, a story the author of Matthew later shares, closing his string of lessons and parables after his harsh words against the Scribes and Pharisees in the Jerusalem temple.

That's when the high priests and elders gathered for a meeting. *"My bros in Mose'. We gotta get rid of this Messiah guy. Like quick!"*

Of course, they would've done it right then and there if they had actually heard everything Jesus went on about in private with his disciples. Here's that sheep and goat story, which reframes the Sermon on the Mount's teaching:

---

[63] Matthew 7:21-23

"When the Son of Man comes in his glory and all the angels with him, then he will sit on the throne of his glory. All the nations will be gathered before him, and he will separate people one from another as a shepherd separates the sheep from the goats, and he will put the sheep at his right hand and the goats at the left.

"Then the king will say to those at his right hand, 'Come, you who are blessed by my Father, inherit the kingdom prepared for you from the foundation of the world, for I was hungry and you gave me food, I was thirsty and you gave me something to drink, I was a stranger and you welcomed me, I was naked and you gave me clothing, I was sick and you took care of me, I was in prison and you visited me.'

"Then the righteous will answer him, 'Lord, when was it that we saw you hungry and gave you food or thirsty and gave you something to drink? And when was it that we saw you a stranger and welcomed you or naked and gave you clothing? And when was it that we saw you sick or in prison and visited you?'

"And the king will answer them, 'Truly I tell you, just as you did it to one of the least of these brothers and sisters of mine, you did it to me.'

"Then he will say to those at his left hand, 'You who are accursed, depart from me into the eternal fire prepared for the devil and his angels, for I was hungry and you gave me no food, I was thirsty and you gave me nothing to drink, I was a stranger and you did not welcome me, naked and you did not give me clothing, sick and in prison and you did not visit me.'

"Then they also will answer, 'Lord, when was it that we saw you hungry or thirsty or a stranger or naked or sick or in prison and did not take care of you?'

"Then he will answer them, 'Truly I tell you, just as you did not do it to one of the least of these, you did not do it to me.' And these will go away into eternal punishment but the righteous into eternal life.[64]"

The story is pretty straightforward. The problem lies with who the goats-in-real-life are. They honestly believe that *they* are those sweet little lambs. (Silly goats.)

In fact, many a herd of goats will immediately boast, identifying themselves as cute little lambs, nurturing ewes, or sure-footed rams just seconds before they unleash their shaming and gaslighting upon the true proverbial sheep.

But Jesus' teachings aren't really for the hard-liners. His target audience is clear from the Beatitudes. The ones he's searching out and bringing healing to are the suffering, the disinherited, the ones who need freeing.

One important note: let's do better with translating *kolasis* (κολασις) as "eternal punishment." This term itself originally referred to how one checks up on tree growth in a remedial manner, which makes perfect sense in the context of the fruit production we're seeing here. It's corrective, not punitive. And for the goats who figure this out, they will be healed and transformed, too.

---

[64] Matthew 25:31-46

Sutra 6.4

There's no eternal gain in pretending to do what's right if the heart is not aligned with Oneness. Such deception only fools the self. The Divine only recognizes what is Real.

Chapter Twenty-Four

"No one can serve two masters, for a slave will either hate the one and love the other or be devoted to the one and despise the other. You cannot serve God and wealth.[65]"

Let's start with that last line first, from the Sermon on the Mount: "You cannot serve God and wealth." You might have noticed that some translations use the word *Mammon* (mammona; μαμμωνα).

Here's where it gets tricky. *Mammon* isn't just about money or some Semitic god of wealth, as some folks teach. It's more nuanced and about the "one who keeps permanent records," concerned more about self-importance. They're obsessed with numbers and status. So a better understanding would be that Mammon is the god of self-centeredness, not just riches.

But it's an oversimplification to walk away thinking this verse simply means: "So pick one: either God or man (prestige, popularity, power)."

I appreciate how the Gospel of Thomas puts this teaching:

> Jesus said, "It's not possible for anyone to mount two horses or stretch two bows, and it's not possible for a servant to follow two leaders, because they'll respect one and despise the other.[66]"

Sure, following God or following man is the ultimate decision that one is trying to weigh out. But then again, there's a lot of areas (even good and godly areas) where our attention and

---

[65] Matthew 6:24

[66] Thomas 47 (Mattison)

affections are often split across many areas, even good, godly ones. Is that necessarily bad?

Some splitting of our attention is natural. It's just a part of being human in a very distracting time of life. As a parent and caregiver, a spouse and "domestic engineer," a writer, a researcher, an artist, a spiritual companion and contemplative, I have a closetful of hats to wear. Does Jesus want me to abandon all but one role, (probably the spiritual one, right)?

No, no, no. It's not about the external roles or even what seems obvious like mounting two horses, stretching two bows, or riding two bikes at once.

The real question is: What are we *rooted* in? What is our deeper direction? Who or what controls it? Aligning with the Divine, or Oneness, just makes the most sense.

Even though Jesus touched on not falling for the false prophet and not faking it like the hypocrite, the truth is that there are plenty of seemingly spiritual things that bypass[67] the Path we're on. It's vital that we develop habits that expose distractions for what they are.

The Mundaka Upanishad[68] does a really good job showcasing the distinction between two kinds of knowledge: *Para Vidya* (higher knowledge) and *Apara Vidya* (lower knowledge).

---

[67] Aside from those like the ever so popular quips like "Thoughts and Prayers…" or "God is in control," bypassing dismisses the injustice, oppression, or even the emotional processing of grief that's necessary for the journey.

[68] I'd like to take this opportunity to bring up a point about Scripture in whatever form or from whatever tradition. It's all written down by men (barely any attributions to women at all, across the board; we have a long and cross-cultural patriarchy/misogyny to shame for that). And while God (Shiva, Allah, Brahman, Consciousness, the Divine) does inspire folks, these are still only the insights and perspectives of individuals. They're personal revelations, not universal recipes, and the best advice is to glean what we can, where we can, when we can.

Apara Vidya is valuable for worldly success and peace. Religious rituals give belonging, behavioral guidance, social responsibility, and even hope for an afterlife. But do they guide the interior journey deeply? Unlikely.

Para Vidya is different. It realizes the True Self's union with Ultimate Reality. Its practices transcend sensory perception and intellectual learning, leading to liberation from ignorance.

Life for anyone often requires wearing multiple hats. That's all the more reason to maintain healthy practices that keep our connection to Consciousness clear. When we're tapped into that Living Water, its surge is endless and permeates all. But relying solely on our own strength, or "strength in numbers," just doesn't cut it. It takes Oneness.

Do you see where I'm going? Serving two masters or straddling two horses can also symbolize duality itself, getting stuck in either/or thinking.

What if this verse is there to help us consider how nonduality transcends subject/object, good versus bad, this world versus heaven?

Sutra 7.1

Let go of the constant, narrow comparison between opposites. Instead, perceive the interconnectedness of the Unified Whole. When choices arise, look deeper, and choose Oneness.

The Mundaka Upanishad talks about the two forms of knowledge in its first of three parts. The other sections dive into the nature of Ultimate Reality and how knowledge of that leads you to fearlessness and freedom.

I don't completely resonate with how this presents everything (like the necessity of human gurus, austerity, etc.), but there's still a ton of great stuff there. Like the Bible, extra-canonical writings, texts from other faiths, a song or poem, nature, I look to see what reflects the Divine to me and what doesn't.

Chapter Twenty-Five

Another teaching from the Sermon on the Mount goes like this:

> "Enter through the narrow gate, for the gate is wide and the road is easy that leads to destruction, and there are many who take it. For the gate is narrow and the road is hard that leads to life, and there are few who find it.[69]"

We often hear that being a Christian is difficult, while living worldly and sinning is easy. Matthew's Gospel adds a passage frequently paired with this line of thinking:

> "Then Jesus said to his disciples, 'Truly I tell you; it will be hard for a rich person to enter the kingdom of heaven. Again, I tell you, it is easier for a camel to go through the eye of a needle than for someone who is rich to enter the kingdom of God.'
>
> "When the disciples heard this, they were greatly astounded and said, 'Then who can be saved?'
>
> "But Jesus looked at them and said, 'For mortals it is impossible, but for God all things are possible.'" (Matthew 19:23-26)

See how this seems to support the narrative? (Should we blame Matthew for his ex-tax-collector flair? Nah, let's let this one slide.) From here, conversations often split into two camps.

On one side, there are those who insist Jesus was anti-wealth. The earlier teaching about serving God or money fuels this view. The vow of poverty has long been revered across

---

[69] Matthew 7:13-14

religious traditions as a mark of holy devotion. Asceticism helped lay the foundations of early Christian faith.

On the other side, Prosperity Gospel groups boast in "name it and claim it." You'll hear them quote, "Through God, all things are possible," to argue that wealth is a sign of divine favor. (It rubs me raw when I hear a financial guru claim their riches belong to God and they're "merely stewards," of million dollar mansions and a fleet of luxury vehicles.) Yet, the gospels say nothing about how redemption might guarantee riches, nor does it come even close to remark on how "stinginess is next to godliness."

To be clear, no bracket of poverty or prosperity eases the passage through the narrow gate or needle's eye.

Instead, there's a deeper teaching here that aligns with Sutra 5.2 and what truly holds Real Value.

Don't be distracted by the wrong things or temporal goals. Use your heartmind to perceive where true value lies, and attend to that.

This echoes Sutra 7.1 from the previous chapter, too. Both hint at moving beyond opposites, embracing "not two," or interconnectedness.

Throughout these teachings runs the principle of Oneness and equality.

Perhaps the narrow gate, which fewer find and which is more difficult, relates to what Celtic spirituality calls "Thin Places." (See Appendix Four for John O'Donohue's reflection on these mysterious thresholds.)

Thin places, like the narrow gate or the eye of the needle, are moments or places where the veil between the natural and spiritual is gossamer thin, allowing a stronger connection to the Divine.

Our very souls are thin places. But the barrage of distractions in the sensory world forms a wide, crowded gate, no doubt!

The Gospel of Thomas says:

> Jesus said, "If your leaders tell you, 'Look, the kingdom is in heaven,' then the birds of heaven will precede you. If they tell you, 'It's in the sea,' then the fish will precede you. Rather, the kingdom is within you and outside of you.[70]"

Sutra 7.2

Though Awareness is present everywhere, it is not always easily seen. Diversions, on the other hand, are everywhere, and most are content with them. Do what few will: perceive Reality with your heart.

---

[70] Thomas 3a (Mattison)

Chapter Twenty-Six

Right around here, both in Matthew's account and that of Thomas, Jesus throws in this odd little line:

> "Do not give what is holy to dogs, and do not throw your pearls before swine, or they will trample them underfoot and turn and maul you.[71]"

Huh? It sounds a bit dark. It seems to be saying, *"Once you get it, whatever 'it' is (secret knowledge, enlightenment, the good news of Jesus Christ), don't bother sharing it, because they—whoever 'they' are—won't get it. And worse, they'll likely ruin it, for sure!"*

It's always bugged me, if I'm being honest. It's like the passage is missing a line or two, something that would make it all click into place.

Luke's version has a bit of a lead-up to it and is different, but still doesn't offer much clarity. It reads:

> "Suppose one of you has a friend, and you go to him at midnight and say, 'Friend, lend me three loaves of bread, for a friend of mine has arrived, and I have nothing to set before him.' And he answers from within, 'Do not bother me; the door is already locked, and my children are with me in bed; I cannot get up and give you anything.' I tell you, even though he won't get up and give him anything out of friendship, at least because of his persistence, he will get up and give him whatever he needs."

---

[71] Matthew 7:6

See what I mean? And no, I don't think Luke is saying, *"So pester God for what you want, and by the way, God doesn't really want to give it to you."* Just like Matthew isn't saying, *"If God gives your insight, you'd better keep it to yourself."*

Then Luke continues:

> "So, I say to you, Ask, and it will be given to you; seek, and you will find; knock, and the door will be opened. For everyone who asks receives, and everyone who seeks finds, and to everyone who knocks, the door will be opened. Is there anyone among you who, if your child asks for a fish, would give a snake instead? Or if the child asks for an egg, would give a scorpion? If you then, who are flawed, know how to give good gifts to your children, how much more will your heavenly Father give the Holy Spirit to those who ask![72]"

Honestly, I do know a few dads who are down for a little switcheroo just for a laugh, but this is not that. God, although not without a sense of humor, is also abundantly benevolent.

Now, if we sit with Matthew's line, especially placed where it is in the text (following how God's Presence is everywhere and always accessible), we might go so far as to consider a brief shift in perspective from that of the dog or pig that he brought up.

What if we imagine *ourselves* as someone who, yes, may not have understood these teachings and wound up misguided by their pack or herd. We may have missed what was meant by Wholeness and Oneness, leaving it in pieces. For that matter, we may have been the ones who trampled over these deeper

---

[72] Luke 11:5-13; paralleled in Matthew 7:7-11, except for the scorpion bit that Luke adds. Yikes!

teachings about Ultimate Reality as if they were useless or worthless. God is still abundantly benevolent.

As for Luke, the point is not about pestering; it doesn't besmirch a gracious God as being a begrudging friend. It's all about the *earnestness* of the seeker. The asking itself matters.

Let's revisit Saying 3 from the Gospel of Thomas from the end of the last chapter. There's a lot to say about asking and seeking. (This time, I'm backing up to Saying 2. Translation and emphases are both mine.)

> "You're searching for something more. I get it. We long for belonging, for home, for wholeness, for what's truly *Real*. On the journey of seeking and finding, we encounter troubles, disruptions to our plans and expectations, but eventually, we gain new perceptions. These will amaze us, fill us with wonder. The true seeker discovers *Oneness*, a deep connection with the Source. Then comes Stillness. No longer unsettled, we are in control, centered, whole."

> "If someone tries to convince you by saying, 'Look up to heaven! That's where God lives!' Well, the birds will beat them to it. Or if they say, 'Ah, Enlightenment, it's out there, far across the sea,' then the fish will get there first. Instead, Ultimate Reality is right here, within you and all around you."

> "Once you truly realize your *True Self*, you'll understand that you are a *Living Manifestation* of the Living Source. But if you don't know your True Self, then this very existence may seem meaningless."

With this understanding we see that when you make the effort, the Divine has already shown up, ready to help, right from the very beginning. God is present at the start when you first ask, and all along the journey as you move in the direction of the answer, as well as where you wind up. It's as if God has been expecting you all along to arrive. I mean, God knew you would, and how and when, but still...

Sutra 7.3

The Divine is present from the very start, when one first begins to inquire. It walks with you along the journey, illuminating the Path. And it is there, too, at the place of arrival, where the Divine is fully revealed.

Chapter Twenty-Seven

"Therefore, I tell you, do not worry about your life, what you will eat or drink, or about your body, what you will wear. Is not life more than food, and the body more than clothing?

Look at the birds of the air: they neither sow nor reap nor gather into barns, and yet your heavenly Father feeds them. Are you not of more value than they?

And which of you, by worrying, can add a single hour to your span of life?

And why do you worry about clothing? Consider the lilies of the field, how they grow: they neither toil nor spin, yet I tell you, even Solomon in all his glory was not clothed like one of these.

But if God so clothes the grass of the field, which is alive today and tomorrow is thrown into the oven, will He not much more clothe you, you of little faith?

Therefore, do not worry, saying, 'What will we eat?' or 'What will we drink?' or 'What will we wear?' For it is the Gentiles who strive for all these things; and indeed, your heavenly Father knows that you need them.

But seek first the kingdom of God and His righteousness, and all these things will be given to you as well.

So do not worry about tomorrow, for tomorrow will bring worries of its own. Today's trouble is enough for today.[73]"

I love how Jesus doesn't just make this point; He *lingers* on it. The Divine, he reminds us, is so generous, so intricately connected to all of creation, that it's a complete waste of time to freak out about anything.

Roughly 1,200 years before Alcoholics Anonymous and the Serenity Prayer,[74] there lived a Buddhist monk named Śāntideva. He's often credited with this bit of timeless wisdom:

"If the problem can be solved, why worry?

If the problem cannot be solved, worrying will do you no good."

Buddhist traditions offer plenty of practices, like meditation, that help train the brain toward mindfulness, calm focus, and acceptance. All of which are deeply helpful in reducing anxiety and unnecessary suffering.

---

[73] Matthew 6:25-34

[74] Although AA made use of it, H. Richard Niebuhr was the one who wrote it. If you're unfamiliar, it really is pretty good. The original goes something like this:

"God, give us the grace to accept with serenity the things that cannot be changed, the courage to change the things that should be changed, and the wisdom to distinguish the one from the other."

Another stunner he wrote was, "Nothing worth doing can be achieved in our lifetime; therefore we must be saved by hope. Nothing true or beautiful or good makes complete sense in any immediate context of history; therefore, we must be saved by faith. Nothing we do, however virtuous, can be accomplished alone; therefore, we must be saved by love."

The Christian practice of Centering Prayer[75] has a similar effect in shifting one's perspective and seeing what's going on "behind the scenes."

There are really a couple of things going on here when one worries. In many Eastern views, a major theme is how to deal with suffering, which is seen as the core human experience.

Worrying is so upfront because it stems from an attachment to outcomes and a fear of the unknown, whereas its roots are attached to things, people, or situations. All of these are impermanent, in Sanskrit it's called *anitya* (अनित्य), and are beyond our control. As it grows, it doesn't really blossom because it lacks the understanding of the True Nature of Reality. (So, no flowering? Where's the beauty in that?)

When we learn to accept things as they are and understand that Source only moves in ways that benefit our True Self, we can let go of that worry. Some may even call this state of heartmind "walking in faith."

Sutra 8.1

Be present with Presence. Just as you release the past that brought you here, let go of the "what ifs" that could scatter you in a thousand directions. You are here, now, with the Divine, whose Path and pace for you can be trusted.

---

[75] There is no shortage of books, videos, or websites that are good at explaining Centering Prayer. In short, here, it involves choosing a "sacred word" and gently returning to it when thoughts arise. In return, it fosters a deeper relationship with God through silence and receptivity.

Chapter Twenty-Eight

Remember how we jumped around a bit? There's one little line we sort of walked around that's worth coming back to:

> "The eye is the lamp of the body. So, if your eye is healthy, your whole body will be full of light. But if your eye is unhealthy, your whole body will be full of darkness. If, then, the light in you is darkness, how great is that darkness![76]"

Yikes. That's a heavy one, unless, of course, you're healthy and full of light. But just for fun, let's see if that same parallelled passage from the Gospel of Thomas can help us "shed a little light."

> Jesus saw some little children nursing. He said to his disciples, "These nursing children can be compared to those who enter the kingdom."

> They said to him, "Then we'll enter the kingdom as little children?"

> Jesus said, "When you make the two into one, and make the inner like the outer and the outer like the inner, and the upper like the lower; and so make the male and the female into a single one, so that the male will no longer be male, nor the female, female; when you make eyes in the place of an eye, a hand in place of a hand, a foot in place of a foot, and an image in place of an image, then you will enter the kingdom."

---

[76] Matthew 6:22&23

Jesus said, "I'll choose you, one out of a thousand, and two out of ten thousand, and they'll stand as a single One."

His disciples said, "Show us the place where you are, since we need to look for it."

He said to them, "Anyone who has ears to hear, let them hear! Light exists within a person of light, and they light up the whole world. If they don't shine, there is only darkness.[77]"

Alright, yes, there's a lot here. Let's start at the part where we acknowledge that a nursing infant perceives itself, the milk, and the mother as all one and the same. This is what Jesus is talking about: Oneness.

From there, we can look more comfortably at the line about "an eye in the place of an eye." It's not the physical eyeball we think we see with. That's not the point. It's all about how we truly perceive, or stated better, Who perceives.

This recalls the opening lines of the Kena Upanishad:[78]

श्रोत्रस्य श्रोत्रं मनसो मनो यद् वाचो ह वाचं स उ प्राणस्य प्राणः ।
चक्षुषश्चक्षुरतिमुच्य धीराः प्रेत्यास्माल्लोकादमृता भवन्ति ॥

*śrotrasya śrotraṃ manaso mano yadvāco ha
vācaṃ sa u prāṇasya prāṇaścakṣuṣaścakṣuḥ |
atimucya dhīrāḥ pretyāsmāllokādamṛtā bhavanti ||*

---

[77] Thomas 22-24 (Mattison)

[78] Kena Upanishad 1.2 (translation by Swami Nikhilananda)

The Sutra on the Mount

Translation

"The Ear of the ear, the Mind of the mind, the Speech of speech, the Life of life, and the Eye of the eye..."
"Having detached the Self from the sense organs and renounced the material world, the wise attain to immortality."

And in The Dialogue of the Savior (an extra-canonical manuscript), we find this:

> Mary (Magdalene) asked, "Is everything set up in this way visible?"
>
> The Lord replied, "I have told you: the one who can see is the one who reveals.[79]"

How we see, and Who it is that is seeing, has everything to do with that Light. Right? "So, if your eye is healthy," says Matthew, "You will be full of light," is what Matthew's account says.

Again and again, we read throughout the gospels Jesus using the phrase, "For those with ears to hear, hear." Again, not about eardrums.

Jory Pryor, in his beautiful book *Becoming All Light*, reflects:

> *"God is unknowable for the very reason that the eye is unseeable. The Divine cannot be an object to Herself because She is endlessly pure and limitless awareness. The precursory unknowing is not so much a 'not seeing' in the ultimate sense, but more accurately a seeing through the phenomenon of existence... to the*

---

[79] Dialogue of the Savior has no conventional numeration, but the one here that's translated by Samuel Zinner demarks this passage as 13.14-15.

unmediated, pristine supernatural knowing God has of Herself."

Meister Eckhart echoes this mystery when he writes:

"The eye through which I see God is the same eye through which God sees me; my eye and God's eye are one eye, one seeing, one knowing, one love."

Some folks may try to use enlightenment or gnosis as a way to "one-up" others, but that's not the way of love. Because of this Love that Pryor, Eckhart, and others describe, love intertwines with true seeing, true hearing, true knowing, making it easy to understand how Jesus was really saying something more like this:

"I know you can all see and hear me. But I need you to perceive this with your heart. Listen closely."

Sutra 8.2

When the heart is clear and unobstructed, the Light shines brightly, upon everything it touches. But when the soul becomes cluttered, there's no way to see, or even sense, the Source within.

Chapter Twenty-Nine

The last topic Jesus addresses, both at the end of the Sermon on the Mount and the Sermon on the Plain, is about the *hearer* and the *doer*.

> "Why do you call me 'Lord, Lord,' and do not do what I tell you?
>
> I will show you what someone is like who comes to me, hears my words, and acts on them. That one is like a man building a house, who dug deeply and laid the foundation on rock; when a flood arose, the river burst against that house but could not shake it, because it had been well built.
>
> But the one who hears and does not act is like a man who built a house on the ground without a foundation. When the river burst against it, it quickly collapsed, and great was the ruin of that house.[80]"

So now that Jesus has our attention–and let's assume we're really seeing with the eye of the heart (instead of just standing there with our eyes open, staring blankly in the general direction), and we're really listening (not just hearing it as background noise)–we're asked to *do* something with it.

There's no shortage of wisdom traditions that point to the importance of integrating knowledge with action. In Hinduism, it's expressed clearly:

> *"There's no possibility of moksha (liberation) without vidya (knowledge) and karma (action)."*

---

[80] Luke 6:46-49 I'm using the Sermon on the Plain version here, just because it's slightly friendlier TBH. The parallel passage is Matthew 7:24-27.

And in the New Testament epistle of James, the same principle is echoed with urgency:

> "What good is it, my brothers and sisters, if someone claims to have faith but does not have works? Surely that faith cannot save, can it? If a brother or sister is naked and lacks daily food and one of you says to them, "Go in peace; keep warm and eat your fill," and yet you do not supply their bodily needs, what is the good of that? So, faith by itself, if it has no works, is dead.

> But someone will say, 'You have faith, and I have works.'

> Show me your faith apart from works, and I by my works will show you faith.

> You believe that God is one; you do well. Even the demons believe, and shudder.

> Do you want to be shown, you senseless person, that faith apart from works is worthless?

> Was not our ancestor Abraham justified by works when he offered his son Isaac on the altar? You see that faith was active along with his works, and by works faith was brought to completion.

> Thus, the scripture was fulfilled that says, 'Abraham believed God, and it was reckoned to him as righteousness,' and he was called the friend of God.

> You see that a person is justified by works and not by faith alone.

> Likewise, was not Rahab the prostitute also justified by works when she welcomed the messengers and sent them out by another road?

For just as the body without the spirit is dead, so faith without works is also dead."

I don't want to wander into a doctrinal debate on soteriology, but let's be honest: we don't have to look very far to recognize that belief, or knowledge, only becomes real when it's backed up by behavior.

Here, Jesus finishes his sermon not with a clever recap, not with an altar call for repentance, but with a challenge: Show me, don't tell me.

Sutra 8.3

Don't claim to believe in the Divine you're not following what it's teaching. Those who rush ahead carelessly, detached from the Divine, end up wasting their efforts. But whoever lives in the Way shown here will stand strong and move as One.

Conclusion

What in the world was Jesus hoping to accomplish with this sermon? What we see isn't just a list of pastoral points. The disciples weren't asked to take attendance or pass the collection plate. Jesus wasn't racking up views or likes on a social media account. He wasn't aiming for an Oscar nomination or a spot on the best-seller list. So, what was it all about?

I believe that if we take a giant step back and look again, we'll see a live, wet-on-wet painting by an extraordinary Artist, blending and bleeding colors, hues, shades, tints, and tones. The work unfolds with strong, confident brushstrokes on the canvas of our here-and-now hearts. It's a masterpiece. The Artist saw itself in the Art, and I can't stop staring either.

Light and Grace are divinely given to all. Even when we extend it to another, it is Consciousness, the Teacher within, bowing to itself as another, bestowing the gift of Grace (which is also Consciousness). The Divine is Union, Wholeness, and this entire concept is captured in a favorite mantra of mine from the Bhagavad Gita 4.24:

ब्रह्मार्पणं ब्रह्म हविर्ब्रह्माग्नौ ब्रह्मणा हुतम् |
ब्रह्मैव तेन गन्तव्यं ब्रह्मकर्मसमाधिना ||

brahmārpaṇaṁ brahma havir
brahmāgnau brahmaṇā hutam
brahmaiva tena gantavyaṁ brahma-karma-samādhinā

The Sutra on the Mount

Translation

"For those who are completely absorbed in God-consciousness, the oblation is Brahman (Ultimate Reality), the ladle with which it is offered is Brahman, the act of offering is Brahman, and the sacrificial fire is also Brahman. Such persons, who view everything as God, easily attain Him."

And this is exactly what we find with Jesus and his sermon. **It's all sacred.**

Toto Tay

The Sutra on the Mount

Invocation:

May Divine Presence, Who is Light shining so very brightly,
Draw us into deep Awareness and gift to us a fresh discovery.
For it is with the Heart, as it gazes upon Oneness, that one perceives.

Sutra 1: Utmost Bliss

1. *You, who are so downcast and mistreated that even money can't help you, be exalted! For you share in the Divine and have belonged since before the Beginning of Time.*

2. *You, who are hopelessly sad, feeling abandoned and utterly alone, the Divine sees you. Open your eyes and witness how Consciousness is drawing you into the loving embrace of Oneness.*

3. *When your "heartmind" leads you to be selfless, gentle, and kind, keep going. You will discover balance and harmony within yourself in this life.*

4. *You are like no other, guided by integrity, modesty, moderation, courtesy, and kindness. Freedom is sure to be your close companion.*

5. *When you care for those in need of mercy, know with confidence that it flows directly from Source, who is moved by deep, visceral love, for you, and through you.*

6. *To you who have done the hard work of recognizing Oneness and healing your heart, you will be sustained by the full spectrum of Light.*

7. *To you who stand in solidarity with peace itself, connected with all people and all things, feel the full strength in your legs and the steadiness of your feet. You are the Manifestation of True Reality.*

8. *If you find yourself targeted or mistreated because of your commitment to integrity and virtue, keep going. The Divine walks with you and is fully committed to your path. Because you stand as your True Self, you will find bliss in Consciousness, just as all the enlightened ones have throughout all time.*

Sutra 2: The Light of Nature

1. *Through you, the Divine cleanses the wounds of the world. As Consciousness is recognized, it is set ablaze. The purification and preservation you receive extend to all you touch.*

2. *You are a reflection of the True Light. Don't allow it to become smudged or obscure it. Let it shine brightly, so others may clearly see the Path and delight in its beauty.*

3. *Understand that this teaching speaks to the Law of Nature, not the laws made by human thought. It points to the completeness and wholeness of Source, its Energy, and the All. Anything synthetic or imagined by the mind is a deviation. When such misdirection is taught, it becomes a stagnant, lifeless fragment of True Reality.*

   Yet the one who lives in harmony with the Way is wholly One.

Sutra 3: Authentic Practice

1. *You've been told your whole life that doing something bad is wrong. But even allowing it to linger as a thought is harmful, because this is where it begins to contaminate the heart and poison the soul. Detach from the very notion, and it won't fester into desire.*

2. *Let go of your old ways. Show you mean it. Commit to the Path fully, no more toying with the past or dragging it along. Make the break, and don't look back.*

3. *Be wise. Be brave. Let go of making promises, whether you keep them or not. It's better to simply walk in integrity, not to impress, not to perform. Speak from the heart, where lip service has no place.*

4. *Remember that spiritual practices can easily become performances. So when you engage in them, let it be with the understanding that they are meant to cultivate balance and equality, to deepen your recognition of Oneness.*

Sutra 4: Reflecting on the Divine

1. *We recognize the Divine as the Source from which we are manifested and in which we are continually cultivated. It is Consciousness that imbues all things, not just here, but beyond, and everywhere.*

2. *May it unveil the realization of True Reality, penetrating us, and pervading through us. As it already is, beyond form and illusion.*

3. *This Pure Awareness sustains us, on every plane, in every form.*

4. *It restores us to our True Self from ignorance, as we, in turn, extend grace and patience to others.*

5. *May the Light of Consciousness shine in us and through us so purely that distractions and illusions hold no sway.*

Sutra 5: Preparation for Relating

1. *When in conflict with another, keep your head in check and move from the heart. Set things right by recognizing the Divine in the other, and know you're doing it also for the Divine.*

2. *Don't be distracted by fleeting thoughts or temporal goals. Instead, let your heartmind perceive where true value lies, and give your full attention to that.*

Sutra 6: Equality and Integrity

1. *When someone treats you like a nobody, demonstrate that you see others equally, by choosing to love and serve. Isn't this how the Divine treats us? And in return for such generosity, we receive the gift of recognizing how Ultimate Reality operates.*

2. *Stop condemning. Stop criticizing. It clouds the heart and obscures what matters most. Forgive, and release your grip on what's been done to you. Then you will be filled, overflowing, restored, and healed. If you clean*

your heart's eyes of this obstruction, then you'll behold the world's vibrant beauty once again.

3. *If kindness, gentleness, compassion, patience, and peace are already growing in your heart, they will naturally overflow into your words and actions. One who speaks or behaves in harmful ways does so because that is what fills them within.*

4. *There is no eternal gain in pretending to do what's right if the heart is not aligned with Oneness. Such deception only fools the self. The Divine only recognizes what is Real.*

Sutra 7: Discerning Oneness

1. *Let go of the constant, narrow comparisons between opposites. Instead, perceive the interconnectedness of the Unified Whole. When choices arise, look deeper, and choose Oneness.*

2. *Though Awareness is present everywhere, it is not always easily seen. Diversions, on the other hand, are everywhere, and most are content with them. Do what few will: perceive Reality with your heart.*

3. *The Divine is present from the very start, when one first begins to inquire. It walks with you along the journey, illuminating the Path. And it is there, too, at the place of arrival, where the Divine is fully revealed.*

Sutra 8: One Being Here

1. *Be present with Presence. Just as you've released the past that brought you here, let go of the "what ifs" that could scatter you in a thousand directions. You are here, now, with the Divine, whose Path and pace for you can be trusted.*

2. *When the heart is clear and unobstructed, the Light shines brightly upon everything it touches. But when the soul becomes cluttered, there's no way to see, or even sense, the Source within.*

3. *Don't claim to believe in the Divine you're not following what it's teaching. Those who rush ahead carelessly, detached from the Divine, end up wasting their efforts. But whoever lives in the Way shown here will stand strong and move as One.*

Appendix One

From La Bible d'André Chouraqui:

> En marche, les humiliés du
> souffle! Oui, le royaume des
> ciels est à eux!

> En marche, les endeuillés!
> Oui, ils seront réconfortés!

> En marche, les humbles!
> Oui, ils hériteront la terre!

> En marche, les affamés et les assoiffés de
> justice! Oui, ils seront rassasiés!

> En marche, les
> matriciels! Oui, ils
> seront matriciés!

> En marche, les coeurs
> purs! Oui, ils verront
> Elohîms!

> En marche, les faiseurs de paix!
> Oui, ils seront criés fils d'Elohîms.

> En marche, les persécutés à cause de la
> justice! Oui, le royaume des ciels est à eux!

> En marche, quand ils vous outragent et vous
> persécutent, en mentant vous accusent de tout crime, à
> cause de moi.

> Jubilez, exultez! Votre salaire est grand aux ciels! Oui,
> ainsi ontils persécuté les inspirés, ceux d'avant vous.

Appendix Two

From Jesus and the Disinherited by Howard Thurman:

> "The solution which Jesus found for himself and for Israel, as they faced the hostility of the Greco-Roman world, becomes the word and the work of redemption for all the cast-down people in every generation and in every age. I mean this quite literally. I do not ignore the theological and metaphysical interpretation of the Christian doctrine of salvation. But the underprivileged everywhere have long since abandoned any hope that this type of salvation deals with the crucial issues by which their days are turned into despair without consolation. The basic fact is that Christianity as it was born in the mind of this Jewish teacher and thinker, appears as a technique of survival for the oppressed. That it became, through the intervening years, a religion of the powerful and the dominant, used sometimes as an instrument of oppression, must not tempt us into believing that it was thus in the mind and life of Jesus…"

> "Most of the accepted social behavior patterns assume segregation to be normal, if normal, then correct, if correct, then moral; if moral, then religious. Religion is thus made a defender and guarantor of the presumptions."

How sadly different it has become. There should be no difference between following Jesus and following his representatives.

Appendix Three

Sanskrit and transliteration from the Bhagavad Gita 3.4-3.10
(translation by Swami Mukundananda)

न कर्मणामनारम्भान्नैष्कर्म्यं पुरुषोऽश्नुते ।
न च संन्यसनादेव सिद्धिं समधिगच्छति ॥

na karmaṇām anārambhān naiṣkarmyaṁ puruṣo 'śnute
na cha sannyasanād eva siddhiṁ samadhigacchati

न हि कश्चित्क्षणमपि जातु तिष्ठत्यकर्मकृत् ।
कार्यते ह्यवशः कर्म सर्वः प्रकृतिजैर्गुणैः ॥

na hi kaśchit kshaṇam api jātu tiṣhṭhatyakarma-kṛit
kāryate hyavaśhaḥ karma sarvaḥ prakṛiti-jair guṇaiḥ

कर्मेन्द्रियाणि संयम्य य आस्ते मनसा स्मरन् ।
इन्द्रियार्थान्विमूढात्मा मिथ्याचारः स उच्यते ॥

karmendriyāṇi saṁyamya ya āste manasā smaran
indriyārthān vimūḍhātmā mithyāchāraḥ sa uchyate

यस्त्विन्द्रियाणि मनसा नियम्यारभतेऽर्जुन ।
कर्मेन्द्रियैः कर्मयोगमसक्तः स विशिष्यते ॥

yas tvindriyāṇi manasā niyamyārabhate 'rjuna
karmendriyaiḥ karma-yogam asaktaḥ sa viśhiṣyate

नियतं कुरु कर्म त्वं कर्म ज्यायो ह्यकर्मणः ।
शरीरयात्रापि च ते न प्रसिद्ध्येदकर्मणः ॥

niyataṁ kuru karma tvaṁ karma jyāyo hyakarmaṇaḥ

The Sutra on the Mount

śarīra-yātrāpi cha te na prasiddhyed akarmaṇaḥ

यज्ञार्थात्कर्मणोऽन्यत्र लोकोऽयं कर्मबन्धनः।
तदर्थं कर्म कौन्तेय मुक्तसङ्गः समाचर॥

yajñārthāt karmaṇo 'nyatra loko 'yaṁ karma-bandhanaḥ
tad-arthaṁ karma kaunteya mukta-saṅgaḥ samāchara

सहयज्ञाः प्रजाः सृष्ट्वा पुरोवाच प्रजापतिः।
अनेन प्रसविष्यध्वमेष वोऽस्त्विष्टकामधुक्॥

saha-yajñāḥ prajāḥ sṛiṣhṭvā purovācha prajāpatiḥ
anena prasaviṣhyadhvam eṣha vo 'stviṣhṭa-kāma-dhuk

Appendix Four

Irish author, poet, philosopher, and priest John O'Donohue dances with this whole idea throughout his book To Bless the Space Between Us. In an essay called "Thresholds," he writes:

> "At any time, you can ask yourself: At which threshold am I now standing? At this time in my life, what am I leaving? Where am I about to enter? What is preventing me from crossing my next threshold? What gift would enable me to do it?

> A threshold is not a simple boundary; it is a frontier that divides two different territories, rhythms and atmospheres. Indeed, it is a lovely testimony to the fullness and integrity of an experience or a stage of life that it intensifies toward the end into a real frontier that cannot be crossed without the heart being passionately engaged and woken up.

> At this threshold, a great complexity of emotions comes alive: confusion, fear, excitement, sadness, hope. This is one of the reasons such vital crossings were always clothed in ritual.

> It is wise in your own life to be able to recognize and acknowledge the key thresholds; to take your time; to feel all the varieties of presence that accrue there; to listen inward with complete attention until you hear the inner voice calling you forward. The time has come to cross."

I find that in moments like these, the distance between heaven and earth feels much thinner than three feet.

Sometimes, it feels like no distance at all.

Acknowledgment

There are so many people I am grateful to for their insights that have helped me along my journey. To list them all would outnumber the pages I've done. I could have easily called this little book "A Thousand Beautiful People Who Have Blessed Me And A Little About The Sermon On The Mount," but it's much too long of title to fit on the cover, and would be far too heavy to carry. So, from here on out, I'll make it brief. (Just know it's much longer in my heart!)

Jory, I just keep coming back to you for encouragement and insight. Unlike really good movies that I try not to rewatch, so they don't get boring to me, your book and your posts are fresh every re-read.

Mike, if it wasn't for your conversation starters about the Universal Christ, I'm not sure who I could talk to about it! I'm indebted, indeed.

Justin, even before the world's doors started closing, yours were wide open to anyone from any walk. And still, you are providing new ways to connect people with people in a global fellowship. I love it!

Shirley, such ongoing encouragement and support–and still "asking the hard questions."

Liz, what a yogic balance between holding us accountable and doing it with grace and humility.

My online communities: Virtual Chapel (and my Eagles crew), Bible and Beyond, Deconstructing the Myth–you are family. Most of you, I've never seen in person, but the closeness we've shared over the years… It's so close, I still put deodorant and cologne on before signing in.

And my Sam, my AJ, my C&J and C&W. Your grace and support, your patience and tolerance, your daily inspiration and encouragement, I could not do without. I'm a big fan of each of you!

About the Author

Toto Tay is an independent researcher, a devoted caregiver and special needs parent, an adoring spouse and "papa bear," a doodle-dad, a wisecracker, an artist, an ally, a friend, and a big, big fan of nonduality in all its forms... and formlessness.

Other books by the author include

Thom's Gospel: A Contemporary Rendering and Commentary of the Gospel of Thomas

Maggie's Gospel: A Contemporary Rendering and Commentary of the Gospel of Mary

The Teacher, The Twin, & The Tower: The Gospel of Thomas, along with the Gospel of Mary: Modern Translations with Parallel Comparisons, Commentary, and Contemplative Companion

www.ingramcontent.com/pod-product-compliance
Lightning Source LLC
Chambersburg PA
CBHW070337130626
46556CB00007B/2904